VISUAL IMAGE DESIGN

GRAPHIC DESIGN SERIES
R&H
VOL.1

RESTAURANTS & HOTELS

ARTPOWER
Greatea

Restaurants & Hotels Visual Image Design

Designer: Wang Yu
Chief Editor: Li Aihong

Room C, 9/F., Sun House, 181 Des Voeux Road Central,
Hong Kong, China
Tel: 852-31840676
Fax: 852-25432396

Editorial Department:
G009, Floor 7th , Building 807-808, Yimao Centre, Meiyuan Road, Luohu District, Shenzhen, China
Tel: 86-755-82913355
Fax: 86-755-82020029

Web: www.artpower.com.cn
E-mail: artpower@artpower.com.cn

ISBN 978-988-68243-2-0

Printed in China

PREFACE

Design, the concept of making everyday habits enjoyable, was born in the 20th century. This "luxury" has nowadays become essential–it particularly applies to environments where one arrives as a guest.

A hotel can also be regarded as a product; designing its details also requires such uniformity as designing the package of a beverage product family. The primary aim of restaurants and hotels is to make its guests feel comfortable; therefore, functionality is almost as important as aesthetics, completed by consistency. For the whole building to be entirely uniform, we need to appropriately influence a great number of units by a close cooperation with architects and interior designers. Various obstacles that may arise due to limitations of certain technologies - for example, in case of an embroidered, woven or embossed surface - can easily be converted into advantages by smart and conscious decisions. A respectful attitude can make the designer become a well-informed and multifunctional professional.

The abovementioned conditions act as catalysts; along with our strong professional commitment, they have directed our team towards an ever-active and productive pathway. All commissions and tasks are considered as individual projects, where the procedures of completion and future maintenance and refinement are clearly separate.

In order to enhance effectivity, we are working in groups of 2-3 people within the design studio. The task is extraordinarily complex for hotel branding, as we are designing various end-products, the production method of which is usually different.

Obviously, hotel design also commences with the appearance of demands. The management of the new hotel is usually assembled one year before the actual opening of the hotel; we usually contribute to the activities of the management as external counsellors. In most of the cases sales prior to the opening is of utmost importance, which requires establishment of a realistic, enjoyable picture of the building that is just being built. This impression can convince potential guests and partners to book rooms in advance when the construction workers are still working in the hotel. If all the rooms are booked on the very first day, then it was worth for the client to work with our design studio.

Prior to the actual design activities, it is of crucial importance to collect information on the preferred group of guests as well as on the future style of the hotel. Architects and interior designers can assist us in this respect. Consultations are followed by research activities by scrutinising well-established hotels with good reputation. The demands of our client are compared and contrasted to pre-existing hotels and a series of standpoints are established for design, so that we can exclude the possibility of huge mistakes. For example, a hotel for young tourists close to a railway station must not be mistaken for a luxurious wellness hotel; if we start to develop our design plans towards a wrong direction, future guests may get disappointed. Precise positioning is therefore of utmost importance.

Real work, however, will only start with the design of a logo according to the predefined viewpoints. It can even be considered as a certain kind of experiment, when beyond various criteria, some unique values of the project also have an influence on the result. Things that remind us interesting stories can often be more inspiring than the building itself. For instance, in case of Zara Hotel the Middle-Eastern origins of the owner; while in case of Opera Garden the characteristic nineteenth-century motifs of the renovated building provided us inspiration.

The concept of "bring the building out of the building" is of utmost importance, for by the time the guest actually gets to the building, he or she has already booked or even paid for the room and other services; consequently, the decision has been made based on experiences of the product that have been created - at least in part - by us. At the beginning, decision-making is aided by 3D graphics, and later - after the hotel has been completed and open - by spectacular, perfect photographs. The fundamental intention of guests for choosing the given hotel should also be taken into consideration. In case of a boutique hotel, for example, the hotel itself is used as a basis; for Soho Hotel, we have taken vivid and joyful documentary photographs from the close surrounding and combined them with pictures taken from the interiors; while in case of a wellness hotel, services provided by the hotel are emphasized more in the visual appearance of the hotel.

The main concept of the identity is always the dramaturgic line that guests have to follow. Besides perfect functionality, maintenance of continuous admiration and new experiences is also important. The moment when a guest books a room online an impression is also given, which is further enhanced by appropriate photographs. Approaching the hotel from the airport, the very first real impression is the external appearance of the hotel; therefore, it is as important as the registration sheet itself, which has to be absolutely straightforward. The design of navigation signs on the corridors and in the lobby is preceded by thorough and careful planning, local inspections and modelling–at the time when the interior has not yet been finished, preventing anyone from being lost. In this phase, graphic design gets in a close contact with materials and spatial ratios used during the construction of the building. Small gifts, as well as bathroom equipment will refine the positive overall impression.

The consistent thinking and implementation guarantees that tourists visiting our country will leave this country with a uniformly positive image in their minds about the hotel and the overall time spent there–as we are waiting them back!

Dávid Drozsnyik and László Ördögh

CONTENTS

RESTAURANTS R 008-143

160OVER90
008 P.J. Whelihan's

ANAIS LA ROCCA
012 La Marée

CARRIE ANNE SEAVER
014 Blue Ridge Restaurant

CHARLOTTE WARREN
018 Restaurant Saveur

CODO DESIGN
020 Libertine

CESAR CORPUS
024 MS. G'S Restaurant

ENRIQUE GONZALO
030 Okra Restaurant

INDELIBLE DESIGN
032 Eight 1/2 Restaurant

JAVAS LEHN
038 Still Liquor

JAY FLETCHER
040 Poogan's Porch

SO PLEASED TO MEET YOU
044 Tap Thai Restaurant

KNOED CREATIVE
046 Merchant Branding

LEA ZUPANČIČ
048 18sedem3

LINE ARLANDER
050 Restaurant Diverse

LOSIENTO
054 Alba Restaurant
056 Restaurant Blanc, Mandarin Oriental Restaurant
058 Canalla Restaurant

MATILDA SVENSSON
060 Hazienda Restaurant

NICOLE FISCHER
064 Lucier

SÉRGIO ALVES
066 Menu Paris

MICHELLE GADEKEN
068 Iluminar

NICHOLAS AUFIERO
070 Pi Pizzeria

KARENINA "NINA" SIMMONS
072 Vic's on the River Restaurant & Bar

NORTH55
074 One&Only The Palm
076 Urbano
080 Roberto's

ROSALIND ROONGSEANG
084 Jin Thai Restaurant

RUBBER DESIGN
086 Roam Artisan Burgers

METER INDUSTRIES
088 Sauce Restaurant

RUNAR LILLEGÅRD
094 Identity for Renaa Restauranter

SUSANNAH BRIGGS
096 Homeroom

TOORMIX
100 Jaleo Restaurant, Las Vegas

TRANSPLANT
102 Sous les Cerisiers

RUI DIAS / TREH5.COM
106 River Restaurant

UXUS
108 Ella Dining Room & Bar

VINGERVLUG
114 Wandrahm

VIVIANE MOSSO
118 Na Strelaku Restaurant

CAROL RIVELLO AND LEANDRO ESTEVAM
122 Hai Sushi Bar

DANIELLE DUNN
CREATIVE AGENCY

130 The Francescas Restaurant

FILIP KOKOSZYNSKI

132 Exclusive Places

MATEUSZ PIEKARSKI

136 Sielankowo Identity

PAPERVIEW DESIGN
/ LORETTE SHEBAYA

138 Urban

ACCENT COLLECTIVE INC.

140 SEASON Cuisine Pâtissiartism

HOTELS H 146-251

ADA ROTHENBERG DESIGN

146 Shalom Hotel, Tel Aviv

148 Harmony Hotel, Jerusalem

& SMITH

150 Dorchester Collection — Branding for a luxury hotel group

154 John Campbell at Coworth Park — Identity for a fine dining restaurant within a country hotel

156 The Barn — Identity for a restaurant within a country hotel

AMENÁBAR & YÁVAR

158 Meridiano Sur | Petit Hotel

BRUKETA&ŽINIĆ OM

164 Hotel Lone

CARMEN GRISOLÍA

170 Hotel Belensate

MEDINA & GRISOLÍA

176 Posada Doña Pumpa

CRISTINA JUCAN

184 Hotel Chester

DEUCE DESIGN

186 Dee Why Hotel

188 Harbour Rocks Hotel Identity

ELEVER

190 Hotel Milano Scala

ELISSA SHAPIRO

192 Hazelwood Hotel Branding

ENNIS PERRY CREATIVE

194 Hotel Nest

ERIKA MAGALLON

200 Cantera Diez

FOREIGN POLICY DESIGN GROUP

202 Wanderlust, Singapore

GRAPHASEL
DESIGN STUDIO

206 Opera Garden Hotel & Apartments Identity

210 Royal Park Boutique Hotel Identity

214 Soho Hotel Identity

NOISE 13

216 Pesonality Hotels

SALMAN YAFTABADI

218 Melal Hotel Group

TERO AHONEN

222 Hotel Yöpuu and Restaurant Pöllöwaari

THISISLOVE STUDIO

226 Internacional Design Hotel

MANIC DESIGN

230 The Sultan

BEIJING GUPENG GRAPHIC
DESIGN INC.

234 Kailey Hotel

GOLLOP ROCH CREATIVE
DESIGN

236 Radegast Hotel

PAQUI CUELLO, LUCÍA HERRADOR,
JULIA LAGUARDA

238 The Mirror Barcelona

244 CONTRIBUTOR

VISUAL IMAGE DESIGN

RESTAURANTS

In 1994, the owner of a turnpike-exit, family restaurant in the Poconos wanted to open an Irish pub. After scanning a Dublin phone book for possible pub names, he decided to use his grandfather's name, P.J. Whelihan–a man he knew very little about. Today, this simple Irish pub has exploded into eight wildly popular locations across the Philadelphia and South Jersey areas by virtue of a rather unusual business style: they maintain consistently stellar food and service across all the locations, but they allow each pub's personality to grow organically out of its location. As a result, P.J. Whelihan's means different things to different people, but all are passionately loyal. To some, it's a neighborhood pub, to others, it's a family restaurant, and to others still, it's a sports bar, co-worker happy hour, and all-night dance club. The only problem with this malleable mini-chain was that it now desperately needed a cohesive brand identity that tied it all together without stifling each location's individuality. The brand had to speak to several different communities across several different locations, yet still be the kind of strong, hearty brand you can sink your teeth into. 160over90 discovered a few key facts about the pub's ancestral namesake, Peter Joseph Whelihan–he was a fun-loving, peripatetic newspaperman who loved to drink. From there, we invented an entire mythology around him that embodied the good-time vibe found in every P.J. pub.

P.J. Whelihan's

Design Agency: 160over90

ON MORE THAN ONE OCCASION, P.J. DANCED THROUGH THE DOOR
WITH A SONG AND A SMILE AND A BAG OF
WARM FOOD
FROM THE PUB.

THE OFFICIAL SPONSOR OF THE
16TH ANNUAL WING BOWL
FEBRUARY 1ST · WACHOVIA CENTER · GATES OPEN AT 4:30AM
WHEN IT CAME TO FOLLOWING SPORTS
P.J. HAD ONE RULE:
IF THE ACT OF WATCHING IT CALLED FOR A
NICE COLD BEER
THEN IT WAS A SPORT WORTH WATCHING

THERE'S REALLY ONLY THREE PEOPLE IN THIS WORLD YOU NEED TO TRUST:
YOUR DOCTOR
YOUR BARBER
& YOUR BARTENDER
-PETER JOSEPH WHELIHAN
IT'S HARD TO TALK ABOUT YOUR NEIGHBORS BEHIND THEIR BACKS
WHEN YOU'RE SITTING ON
THE STOOL
NEXT TO THEM
I FIND THE MID-DAY DRINK
TO BE INCREDIBLY
RELAXING
BECAUSE IT USUALLY MEANS
I'M NOT AT WORK

THE PEOPLE WERE HIS BOOKS.
THE PUB HIS LIBRARY.
YOU COULD SAY P.J. WAS A WELL-READ MAN.
In fact, he would occasionally read himself blind.

FROM TOWN TO TOWN, P.J. FOUND THAT EVERYONE HAD A STORY TO TELL.
THEY JUST NEEDED A STOOL TO TELL IT ON.
How long they stayed on that stool was another story...

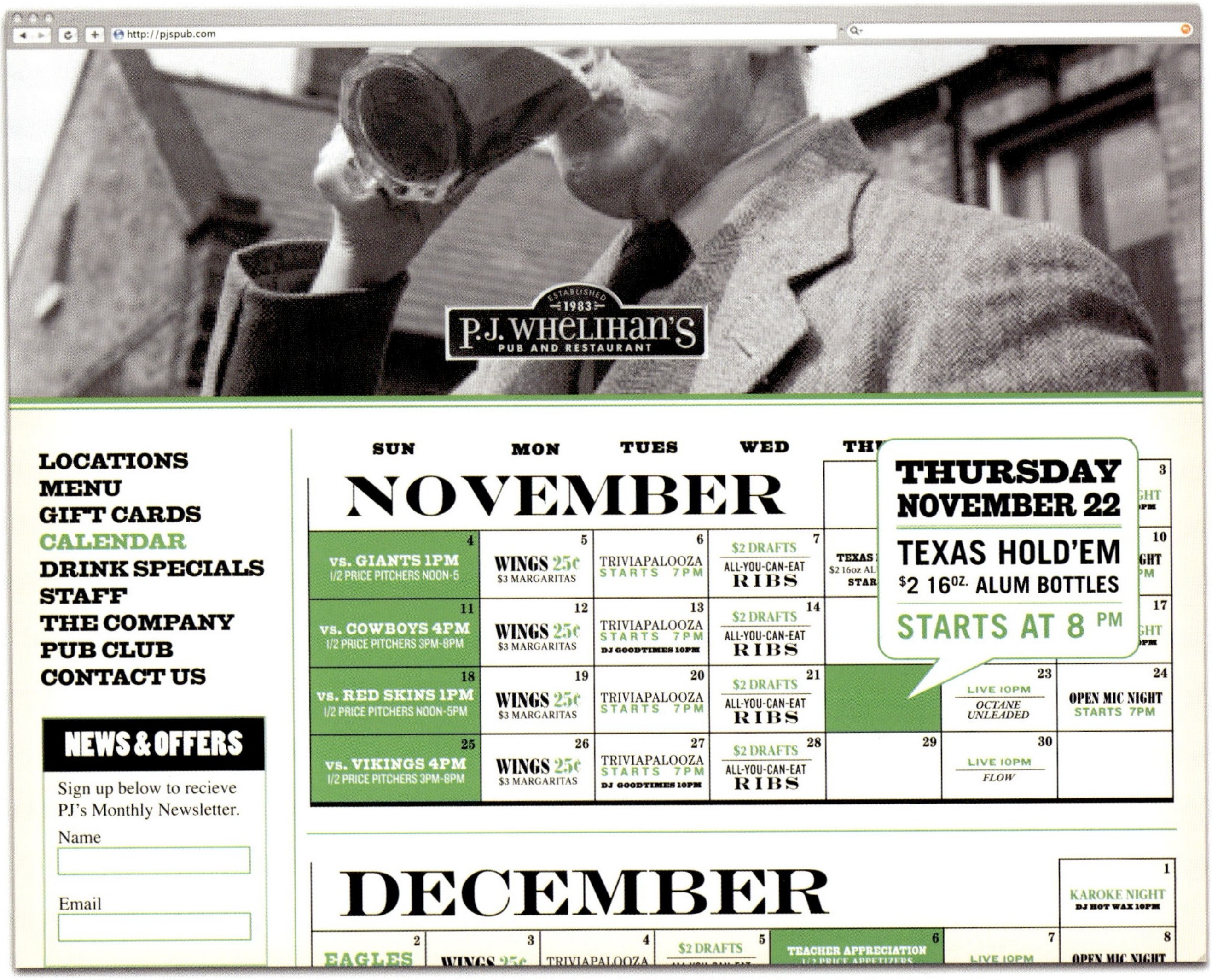
http://pjspub.com
ESTABLISHED 1983
P.J. WHELIHAN'S
PUB AND RESTAURANT
LOCATIONS
MENU
GIFT CARDS
CALENDAR
DRINK SPECIALS
STAFF
THE COMPANY
PUB CLUB
CONTACT US
NEWS & OFFERS
Sign up below to recieve PJ's Monthly Newsletter.
Name
Email
NOVEMBER
THURSDAY NOVEMBER 22
TEXAS HOLD'EM
$2 16OZ. ALUM BOTTLES
STARTS AT 8 PM
DECEMBER

NOVEMBER 20, 1960 WITH ONE CRUSHING HIT, THE EAGLES
CHUCK BEDNARIK
KNOCKED OUT
FRANK GIFFORD
ALONG WITH THE GIANTS HOPE FOR A COMEBACK & P.J. WHELIHAN'S PROMISE OF AN EARLY NIGHT.
A HIT LIKE THAT WAS GOING TO TAKE SOME CELEBRATING
EVERY SUNDAY WE STILL RAISE ONE UP FOR CONCRETE CHUCK.
NOVEMBER

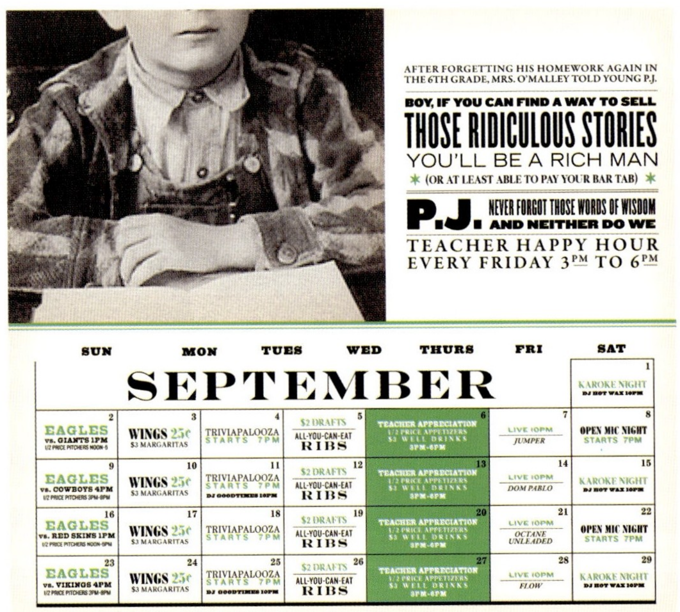
AFTER FORGETTING HIS HOMEWORK AGAIN IN THE 6TH GRADE, MRS. O'MALLEY TOLD YOUNG P.J.
BOY, IF YOU CAN FIND A WAY TO SELL
THOSE RIDICULOUS STORIES
YOU'LL BE A RICH MAN
(OR AT LEAST ABLE TO PAY YOUR BAR TAB)
P.J. NEVER FORGOT THOSE WORDS OF WISDOM AND NEITHER DO WE
TEACHER HAPPY HOUR
EVERY FRIDAY 3PM TO 6PM
SEPTEMBER

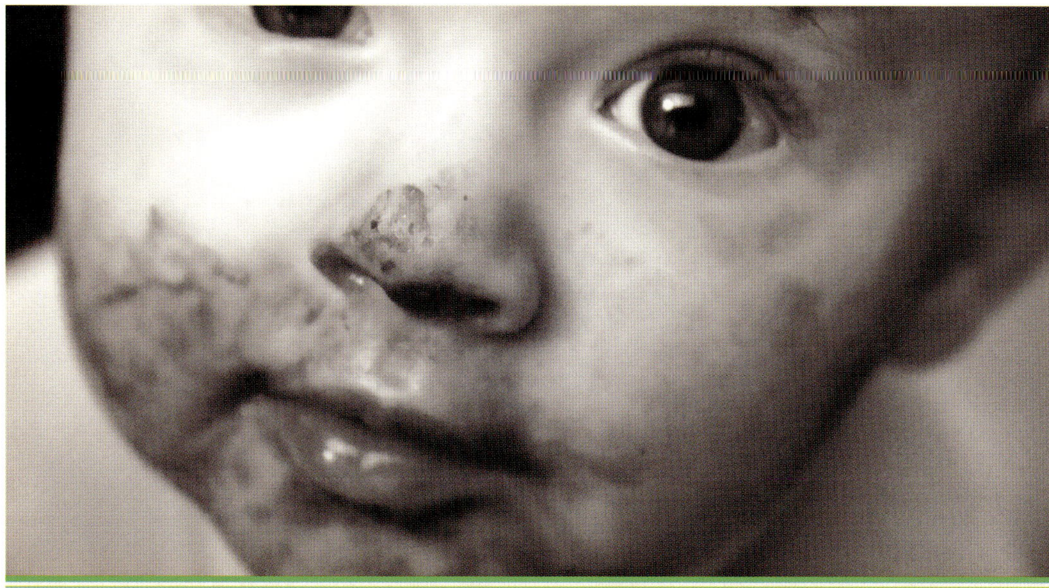

WITH 10 KIDS TO FEED ON A NEWSPAPERMAN'S SALARY,
P.J. VIEWED THE BUFFALO WING AS A THING OF
DIVINE INTERVENTION

WE GIVE THANKS EVERY THURSDAY
WINGS 25¢

P.J. PRIDED HIMSELF ON BEING ABLE TO CHARM A { FREE BEER OFF A FEMALE BARTENDER
IMAGINE HIS SMILE WHEN HE LOOKED UP AND SAW
THE BLUE BELL
{GARIBALDI SISTERS}

GET ALL | DRAFT BEER & WELL DRINKS
2 FOR 1
WEDNESDAYS 4-7PM

Meaning 'The Tide' in French, La Marée is a French seafood restaurant. The design and identity were very influenced by classical French type as well as the illustrative type from old nautical maps. Every element of the design, from the menu and business card to the silver and glass dishes and cutlery reconcile the two worlds of upscale French cuisine and the little seafood shack in the small harbor town.

La Marée

Designer: Anais La Rocca

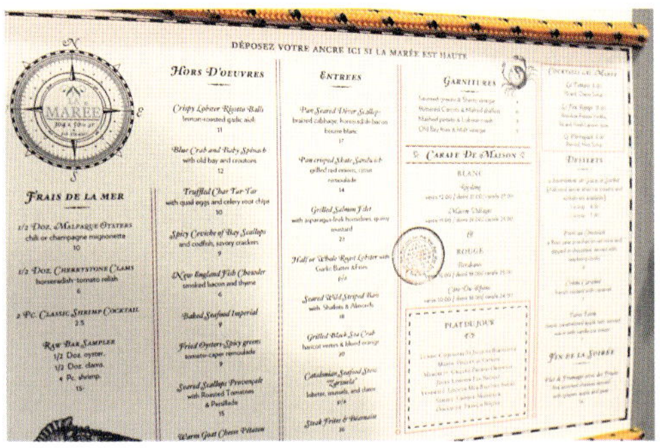

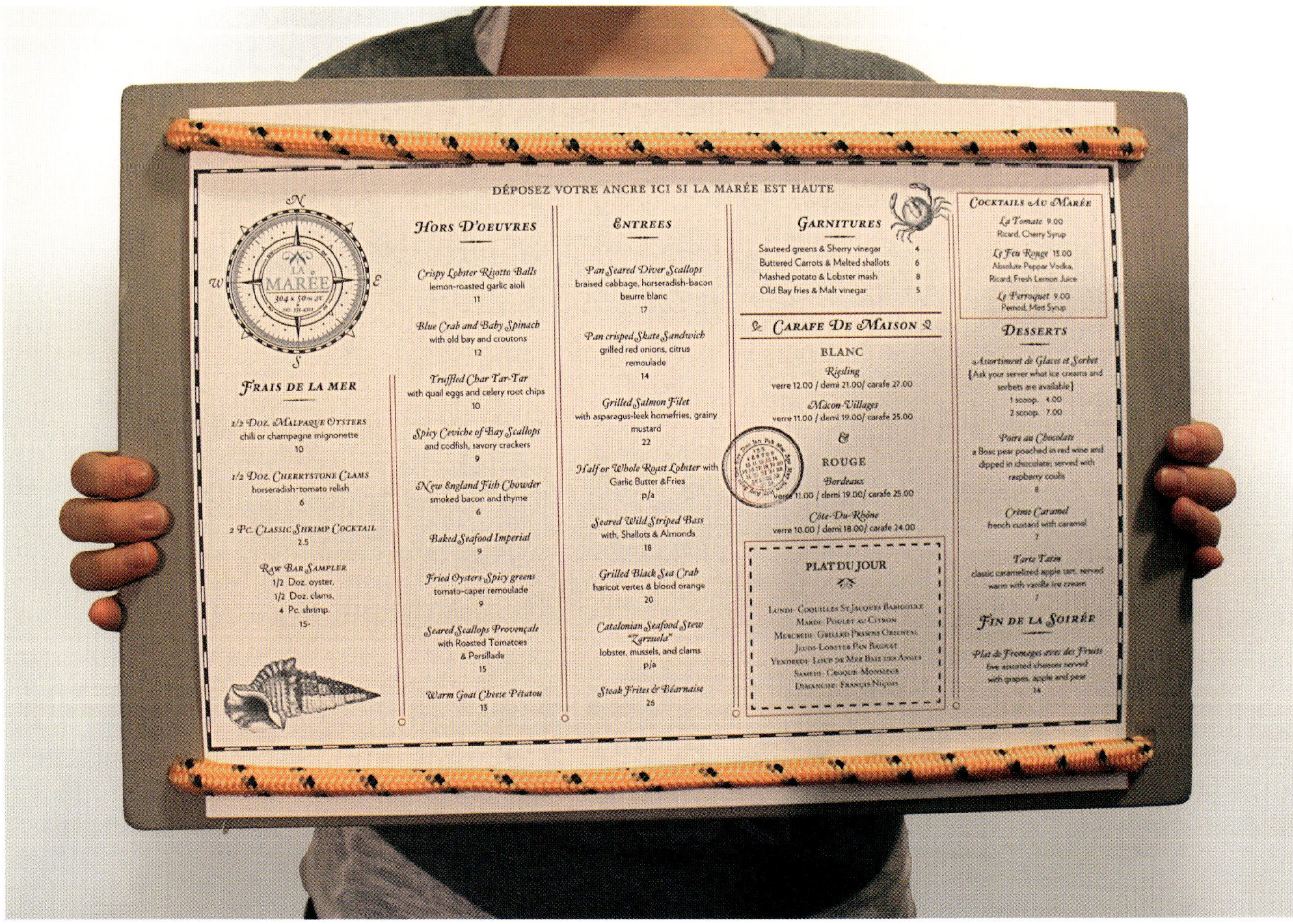

ne
nw
LA
MARÉE
304 E. 50TH ST.
212.555.4321
sw
se

Blue Ridge restaurant is located in the Glover Park neighborhood of Washington, DC. It opened in 2009 and is a neighborhood bar and restaurant offering locally sourced and sustainable menu items.

Blue Ridge Restaurant

Designer: Carrie Anne Seaver

BLUE RIDGE
Honest Food
Honest Drinks
SATURDAYS
9am~1pm
Farmers' Market

BLUE RIDGE
SPIRITS
VODKA
GIN
RUM
WHISK(E)Y
BOURBON/RYE
SCOTCH
TEQUILA
BRANDY
LIQUERS
VERMOUTH
BITTERS
PORT
BLUE RIDGE
SPECIALTY COCKTAILS
high tide
mint julep
pimm's cup
tom collins
gin rickey
silver fizz
mississippi punch
PUNCHES
29 / bowl
mississippi punch
bombay government punch

BLUE RIDGE
BLUE RIDGE EVENTS
events@blueridgedc.com
2340 Wisconsin Avenue NW Washington DC 20007 p: 202.333.4004
BLUE RIDGE
2340 WISCONSIN AVENUE NW WASHINGTON DC 20007 p: 202.333.4004 blueridgerestaurant.com
BLUE RIDGE

BLUE ★ RIDGE

WHITE
chateau de coing tradition millenaire • 2007 muscadet • loire, france
moulin de gassac guilhem blanc • 2006 • languedoc, france
[sauvignon blanc, clairette, grenache blanc]
a clean and fresh white with lively acidity from balanced citrus flavors, accompanied by floral overtones and a hint of apple pie
remy three wives • 2008 pinot gris • dundee hills, oregon

Northern Neck ratatouille
grilled green beans
bacon-potato salad
chicken pot pie
with rosemary potato biscuit, root vegetables
14
vegetable pot pie
with rosemary potato biscuit, root vegetables, mushroom gravy
12
★ OUR MISSION ★
We strive to integrate sustainable practices in all our restaurants:
from sourcing local ingredients, to supporting local watermen;
we seek to do business in ways that benefit our entire community.

BLUE ★ RIDGE
SNACKS
MEAT
ENTREES

I am recent graduate in BA Graphic Design from the Leeds College Of Art., Restaurant Saveur is a proposed restaurant which specialise in chocolate cuisine. I aimed for a luxurious high quality feel influenced by my personal love for chocolate. Chocolate is often seen as a sweet dish however it is also used in a wide range of savoury dishes and so Restaurant Saveur allows chocolate lovers to indulge in this experience. The project consisted of branding the restaurant with a logo, signage, and a main focus on the menu design. As well as elements within the restaurant such as branded uniform, plates, napkins and promotional material such as business cards and a website.

Restaurant Saveur

Designer: Charlotte Warren

RS
RESTAURANT
SAVEUR
Table: 14 Date: 24/05/11 Time: 22:24
1x Stuffed Tomatoes..................£6.95
1x Chilli Pork Ribs......................£7.25
1 x Rib Eye Steak.......................£16.75
1x Choc Mango Chicken.....£15.95
2 x Choc Velvet Pie..............£11.50
1x Peroni...................................£3.60
1x Sparkling Water
RS
RESTAURANT
SAVEUR
Thank You

RS
RESTAURANT
SAVEUR

RESTAURANT
SAVEUR
RS

RS
RESTAURANT
SAVEUR

The Libertine is a classic American cocktail bar masterminded by Neal & Lindy Brown. It's always fun working with these two and even more so when the brand identity includes shades of Americana, cocktail artistry, poetry and what it means to be a Libertine; debauchery and deviancy in both sex and drink – fun stuff.

All in all, we developed The Libertine's identity system, exterior signage, social media art and several print pieces.

Libertine

Design Agency: CODO Design

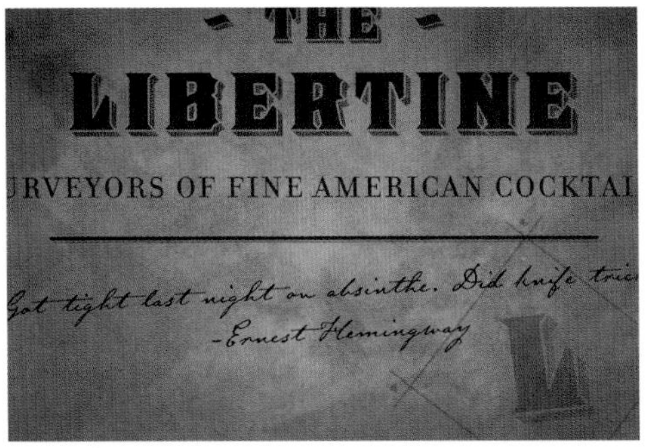
THE
LIBERTINE
URVEYORS OF FINE AMERICAN COCKTAI
Got tight last night on absinthe. Did knife tric
-Ernest Hemingway

BERTIN
OF FINE AMERICAN COCKTAI
X X X
XXX
THE LIBERTINE
PURVEYORS OF FINE AMERICAN COCKTAILS
21 & UP

To the Writers, the Artists, Thespians and Rogues...
XXX

THE
LIBERTINE
LIQUOR BAR
THE
LIBERTINE
LIQUOR BAR

THE

THE
LIBERTINE
LIQUOR BAR

Ms. G's is modern, decidingly Asian and unlike anything you've experienced before. Located on 155 Victoria Street Potts Point Sydney Australia, this Asian fusion bar and restaurant is a four level New York style noodle house and proves to be the new, hip, eat and drink hangout joint.

The quirky concept behind it all was very deliberate and tongue-in-cheek. The Asian mother welcoming you into their home is the main idea behind this eatery while naming the Asian restaurant with letters that spelled a bad rep for Chinese restaurants all through the 80s.

Ms. G's Restaurant

Designer: Cesar Corpus

Client: Ms. G's Restaurant / Bar - (Merivale Group)

Ms G's

A thousand cups of wine do not suffice when true friends meet, but half a sentence is too much when there is no meeting of minds.

REMEMBER TO CLOSE THE FRIDGE DOOR BEHIND YOU

石块击伤人的示意图
天降
妇头
郭思涓・蔡婉婷
联合报道
Ms G's
击破屋顶

Ms. G's

Ms. G's

A thousand cups of wine do not suffice when true friends meet, but half a sentence is too much when there is no meeting of minds.

Ms. G's
WHEN YOU DRINK THE WATER, REMEMBER THE SPRING

Ms. G's

ASIAN MOTHERS ARE THE BEST MOTHERS

CHINESE MOTHERS ARE THE BEST MOTHERS
white fish boiled with half ripe papaya will cause your breast to open up like a tap overflowing with milk.
Ms. G's

Okra is a restaurant located in the neighborhood of Chamberí, in downtown Madrid. Okra is also a flowering plant in the mallow family. It is valued for edible green seed pods. Originating in Africa, the plant is cultivated in tropical, subtropical and warm temperate regions around the world. The logo represents the way the okra looks when is cut in half.

Okra Restaurant

Designer: Enrique Gonzalo

Okra

"La única manera de vencer la tentación es caer en ella"
Oscar Wilde

Indelible designed the identity and website for eight restaurant lounge on 8th and Main St. in Vancouver, BC. We designed a logo, stationary, menus, promotional material, print ads, signage, and website. Our main inspiration was the restaurants fresh local menu and their neighbourhood sense of community. We incorporated that into the project with large images of their delicious and beautiful food and vintage photographs of East Vancouver and graphical maps of the area.

Eight 1/2 Restaurant

Designer Agency: Indelible Design
Designer: Josh Krajina

eight 1/2
restaurant
lounge

eight 1/2
restaurant
lounge
INVESTOR
151 East 8th Ave, Vancouver BC
604.568.2703
info@eightandahalf.ca
www.eightandahalf.ca

Eight ½ restaurant lounge is based on the principle that what goes in to our bodies should be simple, fresh and local. We pride ourselves on having a kitchen that has no need for a deep fryer or microwave, keeping our dishes and drinks healthy and fresh every time.
LUNCH MENU
SOUPS
BREAKFAST MENU

LUNCH MENU
SOUPS
APPETIZERS
SANDWICHES
PIZZAS

COME IN AND TRY OUR NEW MENUS FOR
BRUNCH & LUNCH
B.L.T
Alder smoked bacon, fresh romaine, tomatoes on multigrain
6½
Ham & Cheese
Black Forest ham and cheddar cheese with garlic butter on a baguette
7½
Roasted Veggie Panini
Assorted roasted vegetables and goat cheese with red pepper aioli
8½
Chicken & Brie Panini
Seasoned chicken breast, pesto aioli, brie, tomato, crisp romaine
9½
Tuscan Chicken Sandwich

eight 1/2
About Us
Location
Groups
Menu
Gallery
Contact

eight 1/2
About Us
Location
Groups
Menu
Gallery
Contact
eight ½ restaurant lounge is based on the principle that what goes in to our bodies should be simple, fresh and local. We pride ourselves on having a kitchen that has no need for a deep fryer or microwave, keeping our dishes and drinks healthy and fresh every time.
Check out what people are saying about eight ½—
Vancouver Bars
The Globe and Mail
Martini Boys
Metro
UrbanSpoon
Open—
Monday to Thursday
12pm – 12am
Fridays
12pm – 2am
Saturdays
11am – 2am
Sundays
11am – 11pm
Make a reservation
Availability updated in real time.
More about eight 1/2 Restaurant Lounge
facebook

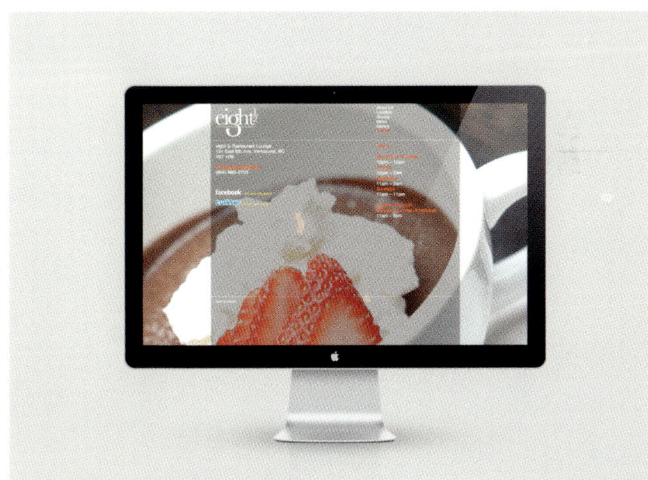

Inspiration for the STILL Liquor identity came from the heart and soul of its location: a 1920's automotive garage tucked away in Seattle, Washington, which sat for years, untouched, still smelling of bootleg liquor. To inspire new emotion from old Americana, the logo was kept simple: The T Model Ford sits in honor of the garage and illegal liquor runs, prohibition era and the heritage of the old automotive garage.

Still Liquor

Designer: Javas Lehn
Location: USA
Photographer: Javas Lehn

STILL
LIQUOR

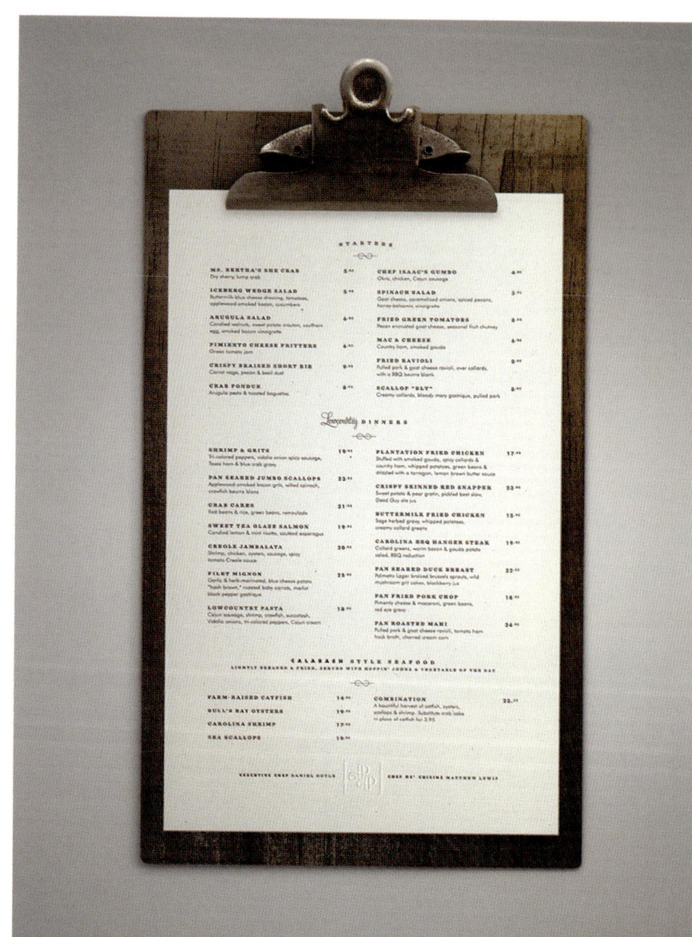

Tucked away on charming Queen Street, in the heart of Charleston, South Carolina, Poogan's Porch is one of the city's oldest independent culinary establishments. Recognized by Martha Stewart Living, Wine Spectator and The Travel Channel, the beautifully restored Victorian house has been a favorite of well-known celebrities, politicians, tourists and locals alike who rave about this Southern institution. Poogan's overhauled look needed to pay homage to their well-known and beloved past, but also offer a fresh, more sophisticated and modernized nod to its future. The project began with the logo and basic identity, then moved into signage, menus, ads, and wrapped up with the launch of a new website.

Poogan's Porch

Designer: Jay Fletcher

Poogan's Porch
RESTAURANT
EST. 1976
HOME THE STORY MENUS GROUP DINING OUR TEAM PRESS GALLERY CONTACT
Poogan's Porch
RESTAURANT

Poogan's Porch
RESTAURANT
EST. 1976
HOME THE STORY MENUS GROUP DINING OUR TEAM PRESS GALLERY CONTACT
FINE FOOD, DRINK AND WARM HOSPITALITY MEAN EVERYTHING TO US.
BRAD BALL
MANAGING PARTNER
A native Charlestonian, Brad Ball began working for Poogan's Porch, his family's restaurant, at the age of thirteen as the delivery boy. Soon after, he became the dishwasher and busboy and eventually worked his way up to server and restaurant manager. After graduating from the College of Charleston in May 2004, he took over as General Manager of Poogan's. Ball traveled extensively throughout the world, including spending a semester abroad in Annot, France, where he developed a keen interest in wine. After extensive study, Ball personally took it upon himself to expand and diversify the wine program at Poogan's, growing the list to 250 bottles, 28 wines by the
some of New York's finest and most respected restaurants. Internships at Jean-Georges, a four star French-Asian restaurant on Central Park, and the increasingly popular Momofuku Noodle Bar in the East Village, gave Ball an edge on the restaurant industry and gave him a glimpse into the kitchens of the industry's best. Perhaps the most gratifying experience of Ball's time in New York came from his time working at Aquavit, an upscale, multi-award winning restaurant. Working under renowned Executive Chef Marcus Samuelsson and General Manager Olivier Zardoni, Ball assisted in the management the restaurant's impressive wine program. Serving as a sommelier for the restaurant, Ball had the privilege of tasting and serving rare, vintage, top-quality wines from all over the world from Aquavit's 350-bottle
Sommeliers. Continuing to challenge himself, Ball completed an executive MBA program with a wine industry focus through the Bordeaux Ecole de Management (BEM) in 2010. Ball hopes to expand and strengthen his business insight by growing his current businesses and engaging in additional endeavors. He is actively pursuing an Advanced Sommelier through the Court of Master Sommeliers and Master of Wine.
Not one to slow down, Ball also launched the La Wine Agency in 2010. The wines produced adhere to a defined set of standards to help show what La Wine Agency believes to be "PROPER WINES," aka un-manipulated, pure expressions of specific varietals or styles that are sustainably produced. The goal of La Wine

Poogan's Porch
RESTAURANT
EST. 1976
HOME THE STORY MENUS GROUP DINING OUR TEAM PRESS GALLERY CONTACT
A SPECIAL PLACE FOR SPECIAL EVENTS
Located on a charming, quaint downtown street, Poogan's Porch offers the ideal setting for intimate breakfasts and lunch meetings, wedding-related activities including bridesmaid's luncheons, rehearsal dinners and wedding receptions and a unique sight for special events including anniversary parties, family reunions, luncheons, parties, etc.
Poogan's Porch is centrally located to all downtown churches, hotels and other event locations. Ample parking is available in a nearby parking garage and the staff is dedicated to making events run seamlessly. An event planner handles all onsite logistics including menu selection, room set-up deliveries, etc.
A popular location for groups of various sizes, Poogan's Porch provides a variety of delicious Lowcountry menu options from which to select. Located in the heart of the historic district, Poogan's Porch is located in close proximity to the Gibbes Museum of Art, the Old Exchange & Provost Dungeon, the Market, the Four Corners of Law, Waterfront Park and all historic houses and walking tour locations. Several area tour companies include the restaurant on their routes, and some carriage tours pass right by the restaurant.
For reservations or to receive additional information about special events and group dining, contact us at 843-577-2337 or e-mail info@poogansporch.com.
VIEW OUR Group menus
GROUP BRUNCH
GROUP LUNCH
GROUP DINNER 1
GROUP DINNER 2
№ 72 QUEEN STREET
MONDAY - FRIDAY
LUNCH: 11:30 - 2:30
DINNER: 5:00 - 9:30
SATURDAY & SUNDAY
BRUNCH: 9:00 - 3:00
DINNER: 5:00 - 9:30
843-577-2337
DIRECTIONS
RESERVATIONS RECOMMENDED
RESERVE ONLINE OR CALL 843-577-2337

HOME THE STORY
WE BELI
seersucker, bisc
grea
BRUNCH
№
DIRECTIONS

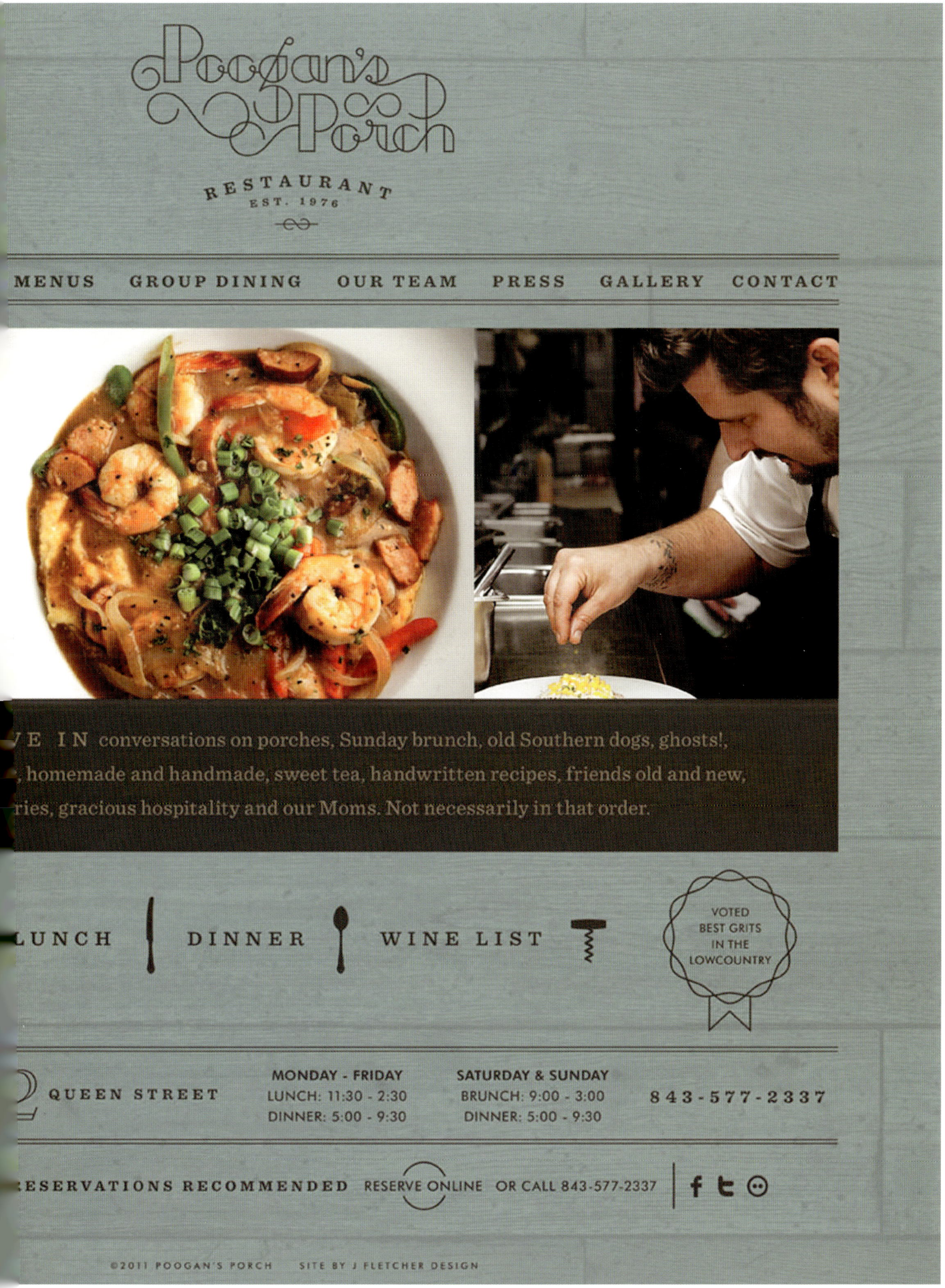
Poogan's Porch
RESTAURANT
EST. 1976
MENUS
GROUP DINING
OUR TEAM
PRESS
GALLERY
CONTACT
E IN conversations on porches, Sunday brunch, old Southern dogs, ghosts!,
, homemade and handmade, sweet tea, handwritten recipes, friends old and new,
ries, gracious hospitality and our Moms. Not necessarily in that order.
LUNCH
DINNER
WINE LIST
VOTED BEST GRITS IN THE LOWCOUNTRY
QUEEN STREET
MONDAY - FRIDAY
LUNCH: 11:30 - 2:30
DINNER: 5:00 - 9:30
SATURDAY & SUNDAY
BRUNCH: 9:00 - 3:00
DINNER: 5:00 - 9:30
843-577-2337
ESERVATIONS RECOMMENDED
RESERVE ONLINE
OR CALL 843-577-2337
©2011 POOGAN'S PORCH
SITE BY J FLETCHER DESIGN

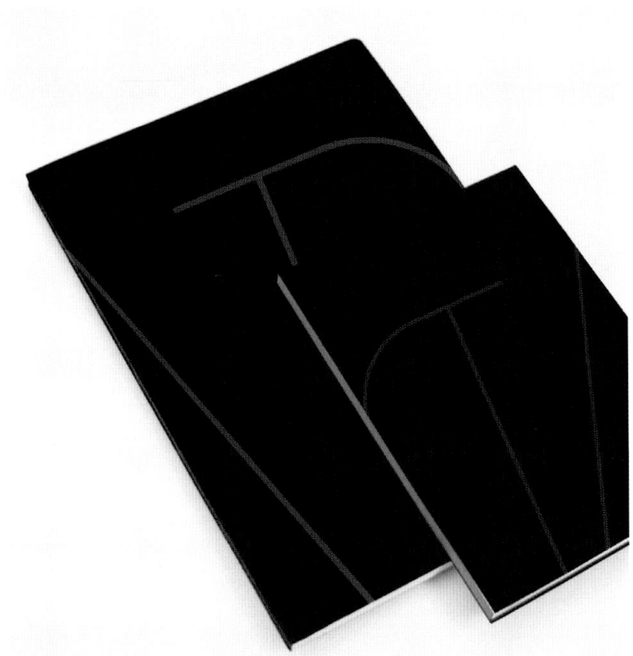

Jennifer Cordova has to create a brand and identity for Tap Thai Restaurant.

Tap Thai Restaurant

Design Agency: so Pleased To meet you
Designer: Jennifer Cordova
Client: Tap Thai Restaurant

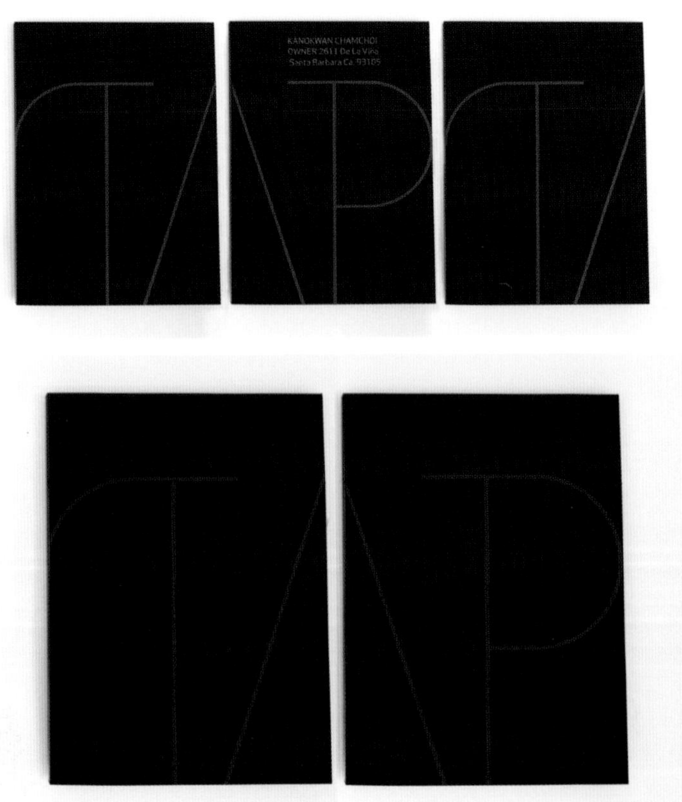

TAP
Thai Herbal Restaurant
PAD THAI
PAD SEE U
DRUNKEN NOODLES
CHICKEN GREEN CURRY
CHICKEN PANANG
TOFU YELLOW CURRY
CHICKEN SPICY MINT
SALMON CHU CHEE
SHRIMP FRIED RICE
PINEAPPLE FRIED RICE
TOFU & GARLIC FRIED RICE
SPICY SEAFOOD RICE
CHICKEN & GINGER CHICKEN & GINGER
VEGGIES & TOFU
PUMPKIN & BASIL

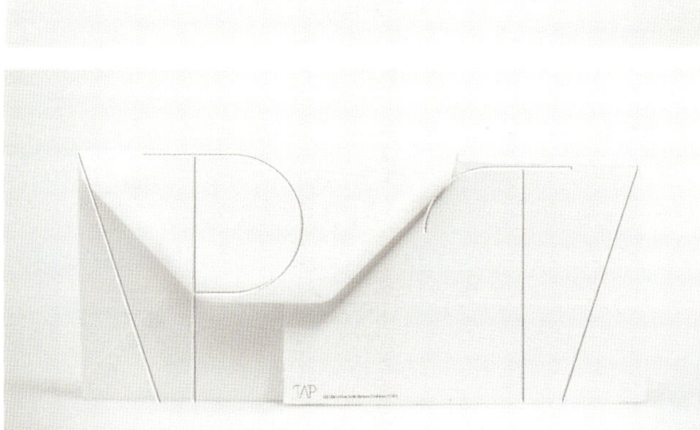

Merchant is Madison's first craft cocktail bar. Serving quality food in a relaxed setting, the menu is rustic and informal. Merchant stands for the way things used to be. A new brand was created with decorative lettering in a timeless crest, preserving and honoring the tradition and craftsmanship of a bygone era.

Merchant Branding

Design Agency: Knoed Creative
Interior Design: fcSTUDIO
Client: Merchant

The brand has evolved from a family run restaurant Kunstelj, situated in Radovljica, Slovenia, which has been serving and hosting guests since 1873. The 18sedem3 is covering sub-brands which are representing a cake shop, catering services, cooking courses, accommodation rooms, wine cellar, local shop and a tourist agency. Despite the complexity of the brand regarding the numerous sub-brands and areas of the its interests and activities, the corporate identity was designed in the principle of logic and simplicity in terms of its usage and the message it communicates. The basic logo can work independently or together with other sub-brand logos depending on the desired communicating message. Another important segment of the identity are the promotional stickers, which were designed in the same visual style as the main logos, so they can be placed on different kinds of packaging.

18sedem3

Designer: Lea Zupančič

18
sedem3
Kunstelj
Ime Priimek
naziv
E: info@18sedem3.si
T: +386 (0)453 15 178
M: +386 (0)40 212 686
F: +386 (0)453 04 15
Gorenjska cesta 9,
4249 Radovljica
Slovenija

www.18sedem3.si

www.18sedem3.si
18
sedem3
Kunstelj

DIVERSE is a high-end restaurant placed in one of the finer quarters in Copenhagen. The concept was a Danish-inspired tapas restaurant, serving food by one of the best chefs in Copenhagen, formerly employed at the well-known 5-star design-hotel, Hotel Skt. Petri. With a cool concept bar, serving delicious cocktails in the corner of the main restaurant floor, and the first floor as a relaxing area with cozy music and lounge, it had great potential for becoming a Copenhagen hot spot. The food alone was absolutely worth a visit, and they received fine reviews, but unfortunately the restaurant had to close the doors after a few years.

The identity for the restaurant was developed to emphasize the high-end feeling, while still conveying some warmth and accommodation. The restaurant and lounge was meant to be a tiny oasis where you could drop in during the day or evening, to take a break. Thus the logo ended up symbolizing a (break), with clean and simple typography and warm colors.

Restaurant Diverse

Creative director: Peter Dalhoff
Designer: Line Arlander

DIVERSE
LOUNGE BAR
RESTAURANT

DIVERSE
RESTAURANT
LOUNGE BAR

DIVERSE
RESTAURANT
LOUNGE BAR
DIVERSE

DIVERSE
RESTAURANT
LOUNGE BAR

This traditional food restaurant has a homey decoration. Therefore, the decision about its identity design was to use the hand made table cloths as a graphic element and to give the logo a clean aspect so that they would coexist in harmony.

Alba Restaurant

Design Agency: LoSiento

ALBA

PARIS

168

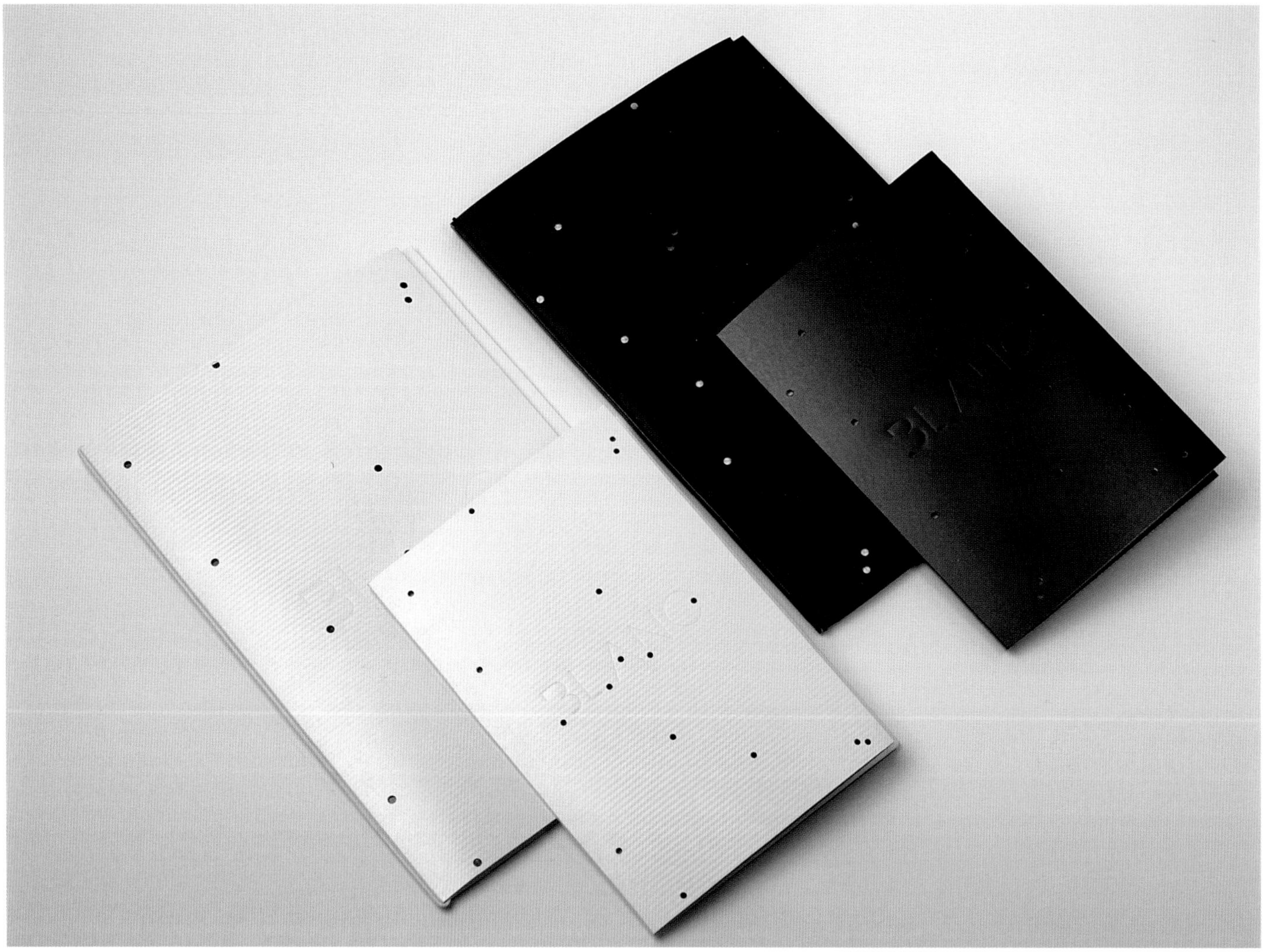

Design of the new brand identity and menus of the restaurant for Mandarin Oriental Hotel in Barcelona.

Restaurant Blanc, Mandarin Oriental Restaurant

Design Agency: LoSiento
Designer: Rocío Hidalgo
Art Direction/Design: Borja Martinez
WorkType: Identity / stationary / Menus
Client: Mandarin Oriental
Photographer: Losiento

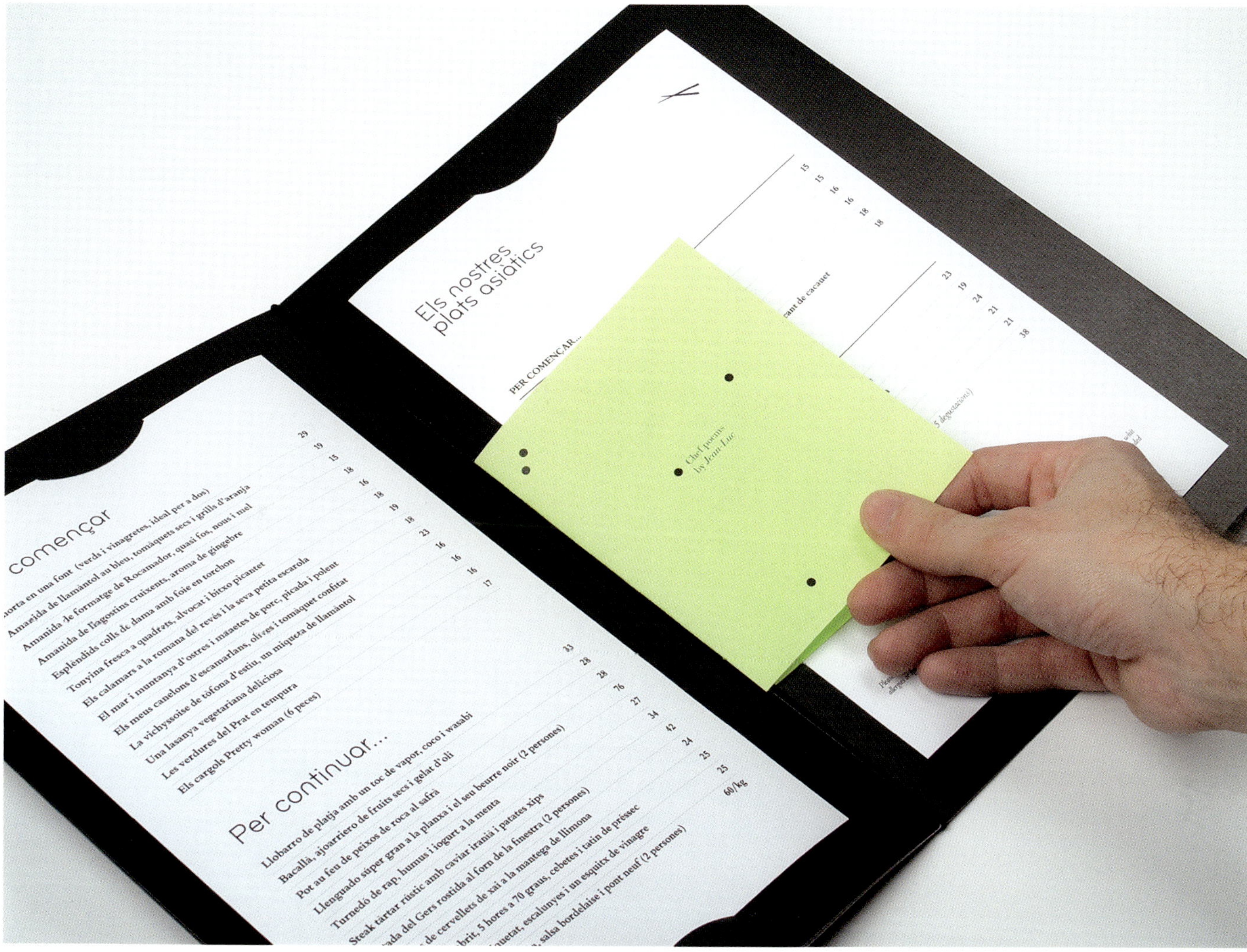
Els nostres plats asiàtics
PER COMENCAR...
començar
Per continuar...
Chef poems by Jean Luc

The particularity of this place is that the space is divided in two restaurants in one: the Canalla is in the downstairs floor and the Villano is upstairs. Since both names can be somehow associated with Mexico, the logo was made to match that spirit.

Canalla Restaurant

Design Agency: LoSiento

El
CANALLA
¡Abajo el canalla!
SAN
TELMO

El
CANALLA
¡Abajo el canalla!
SAN
TELMO
CAFE
SAN
VILLANO
¡Arriba el Villano!
El
CANALLA
¡Abajo el canalla!

Hazienda is a Mediterranean restaurant located in the south of Sweden. It is simple and relaxed, with superb food and a warm atmosphere. The visual identity is to reflect these values: happiness, simpleness and great quality. It has a Mediterranean flair, merged with Swedish culture, so that it appears to be exotic but at the same time appealing to Swedish people. In short: bring out the side of the Mediterranean that they like to see and feel comfortable with. The identity is classy and playful and breaths quality at the same time as simpleness.

HAZIENDA
BAR · MAT

Hazienda Restaurant

Designer: Matilda Svensson

HAZIENDA
BAR·MAT

HAZIENDA
BAR·MAT
HAMNPLAN 2
260 93 Torekov
tel: 0431-364748
info@hazienda.se
www.hazienda.se

PREMIÄR
HAZIENDA
BAR · MAT
30/4
kl 13.00 - 17.00
VÄLKOMNA!
TAPAS
FÖRRÄTTER
FRÅN GRILLEN
BARNMENY
TAPAS
DESSERTER
PASTARÄTTER
Söndagar på Hazienda

HAZIENDA
BAR · MAT
30/4

TAPAS
FÖRRÄTTER

Söndagar på Hazienda

HAMNPLAN 2
260 93 Torekov
öppet året runt
tel: 0431-364748
info@hazienda.se
www.hazienda.se
HAZIENDA
BAR·MAT

HAZIENDA
BAR·MAT

HAZIENDA
BAR·MAT

HAZIENDA
BAR·MAT

HAZIENDA
BAR·MAT

Lucier's innovative Modern European cuisine, high-design environment and uniquely personal service demanded an equally distinctive identity. Using the stamp element from the logo as a unifying graphic element, I pushed the limits of print production for business cards, invitations, media folders and other items with five to seven spot colors and varnishes per side, plus die cuts. Each menu jacket features a handmade glass version of the stamp produced by a local artist.

Lucier

Designer: Nicole Fischer

Lucier

Lucier

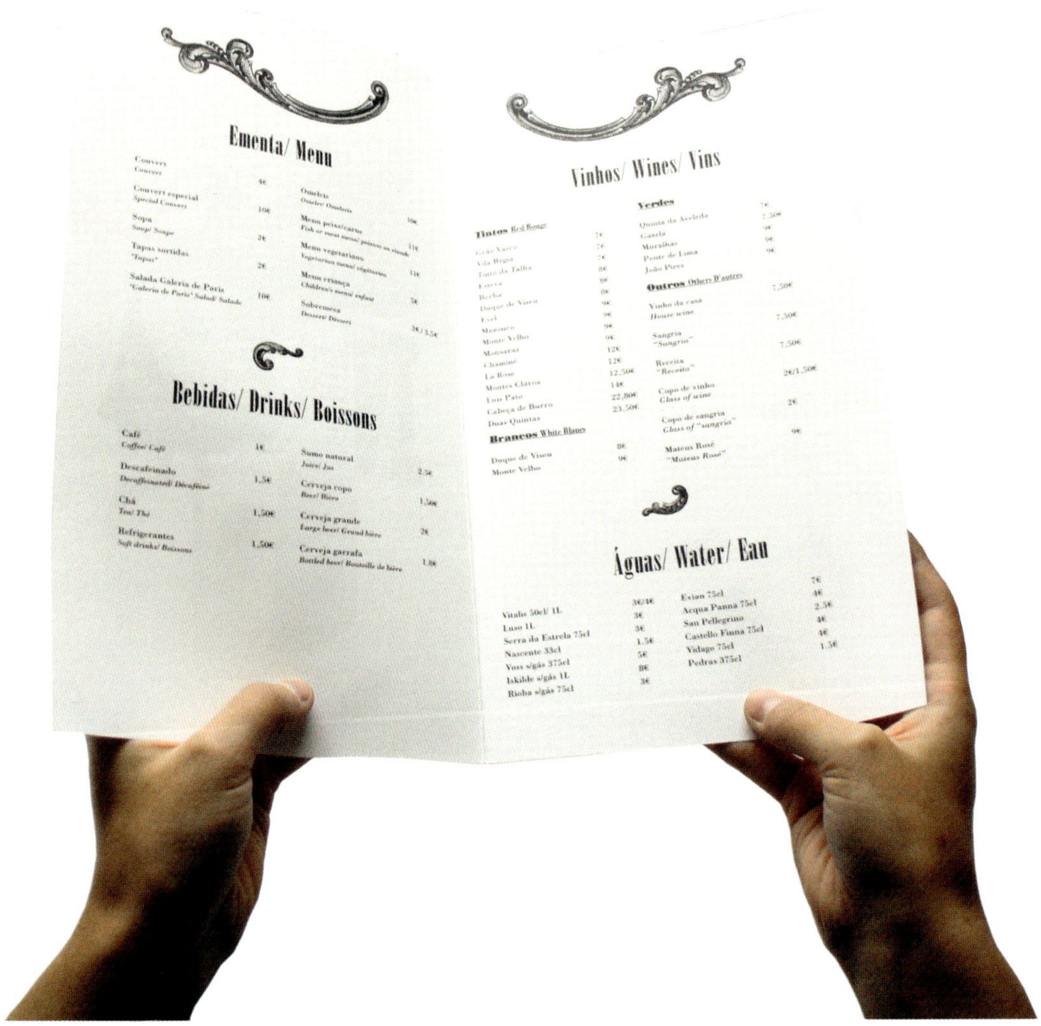

This menu was been made for a restaurant/bar called "Galeria de Paris" in the downtown of Porto. It's a place with retro decorative style with a lot of wood and amazing old objects, almost like a museum. So, it was obvious the menu must have that visual style. After some research and collect a few types and images, I finally select some old wood type and ornaments to make the final design.

Menu Paris

Designer: Sérgio Alves
Client: Galeria de Paris

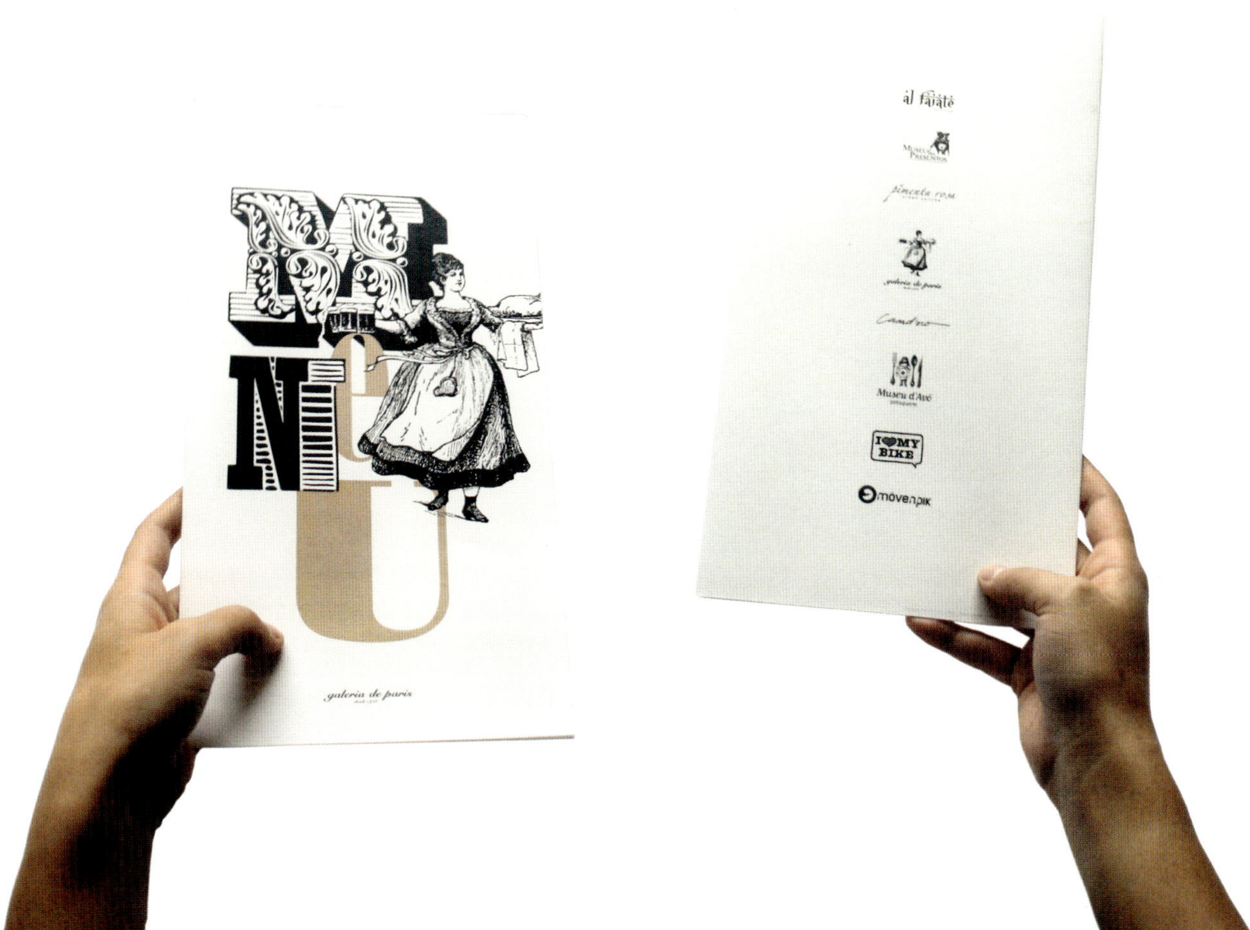

Iluminar is a fine dining restaurant and bar that serves Spanish and Mexican inspired cuisine. Its name, meaning to illuminate, shine light upon, or light up, is meant to instill thoughts of a warm and welcoming environment, steeped in intimate and festive ambiance. The identity strives to accomplish the same while holding a balance between sophistication and rustic flare, employing the use of gold leaf and illustrative details The project included the design and development of a restaurant concept, identity and accompanying business collateral, a menu, and an extension of restaurant décor in the form candle votives.

Iluminar

Designer: Michelle Gadeken

ILUMINAR
ANTOJITOS

ILUMINAR

Known for their traditional Italian foods and strong ties to ancestral roots, Pi Pizzeria is a family-owned, gourmet restaurant. This project includes the design of a mark, identity system, branded material and restaurant products. The identity was inspired by the art of the Renaissance at the beginning of the sixteenth century.

Pi Pizzeria

Designer: Nicholas Aufiero

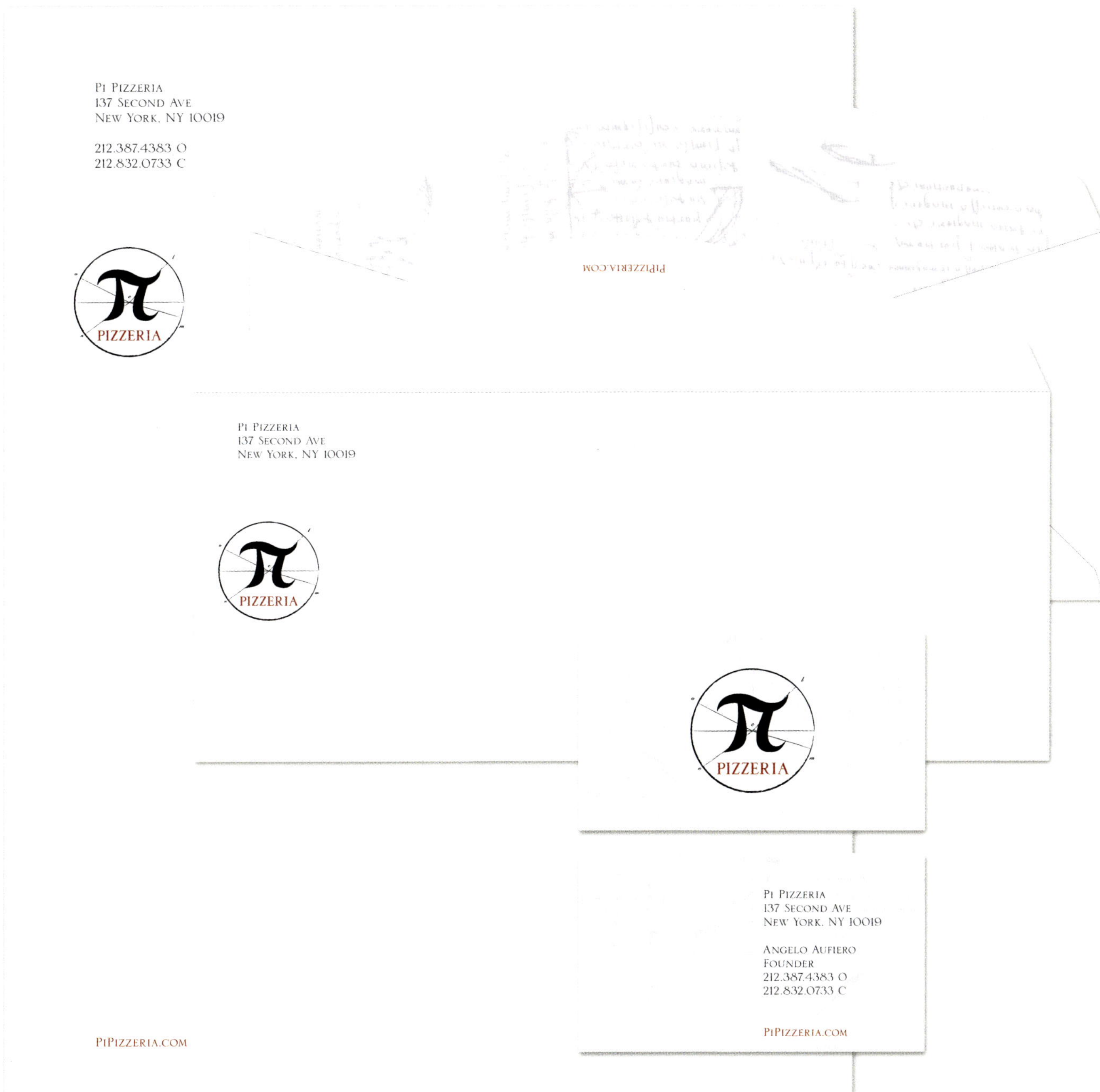
Pi Pizzeria
137 Second Ave
New York, NY 10019
212.387.4383 O
212.832.0733 C
PIZZERIA
PiPizzeria.com
Pi Pizzeria
137 Second Ave
New York, NY 10019
PIZZERIA
PIZZERIA
Pi Pizzeria
137 Second Ave
New York, NY 10019
Angelo Aufiero
Founder
212.387.4383 O
212.832.0733 C
PiPizzeria.com

Objective

Rebrand and promote Vic's on the River Restaurant & Bar, a fine dining restaurant, which specializes in contemporary southern cuisine.

Solution

Establishing a strong identity in the local community is key. I focused on increasing customer awareness with a simple yet bold logo design. As well as showcasing how unique, exciting and friendly the restaurant is with some print ads. All of these elements help to explain who Vic's is and what they can do. Internet advertising is a huge part of the strategy with the creation of a website.

Most people turn to the web when looking to dine out. They need to see an appealing menu, an attractive atmosphere and are very interested in seeing what previous customers have to say about their dining experience. The goal is to present a combination of excellent and interesting food in an environment that appeal to a wide and varied group of successful people.

Vic's on the River Restaurant & Bar

Designer: Karenina "Nina" Simmons

ABOUT VIC'S
MENUS & WINELISTS
PRIVATE PARTIES
UPCOMING EVENTS
CONTACT
VIC'S
ON THE RIVER
View Our Photos
MAKE A RESERVATION

ENVISION
BUSINESS
MEETINGS LIKE
NO OTHER
VIC'S
www.vicsontheriver.com

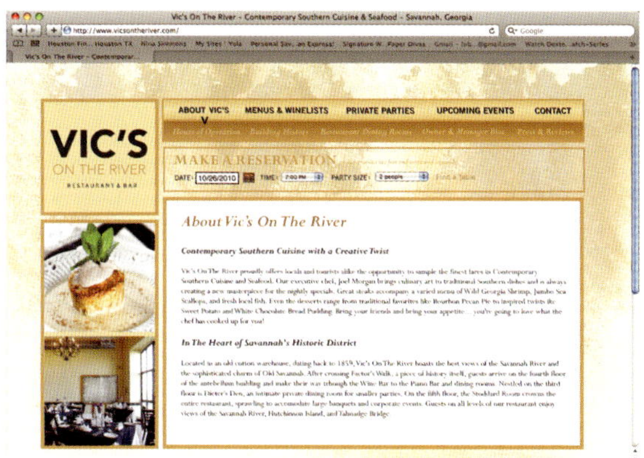
ABOUT VIC'S
MENUS & WINELISTS
PRIVATE PARTIES
UPCOMING EVENTS
CONTACT
VIC'S
ON THE RIVER
MAKE A RESERVATION
About Vic's On The River
Contemporary Southern Cuisine with a Creative Twist
In The Heart of Savannah's Historic District

IMAGINE
SERVICE
YOU CAN'T FIND
ANYWHERE
VIC'S
www.vicsontheriver.com

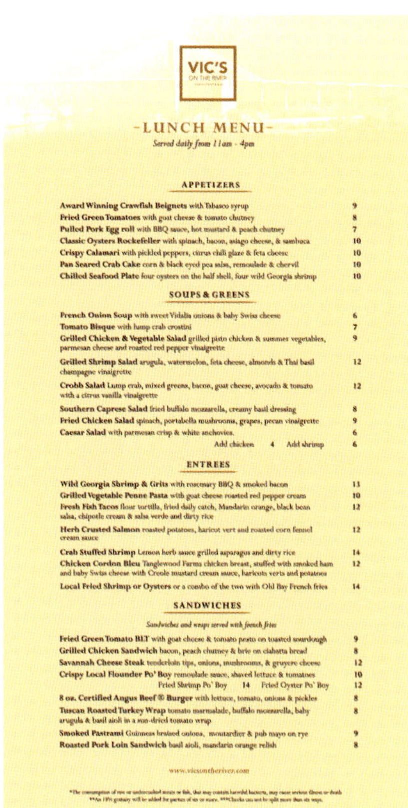
VIC'S
-LUNCH MENU-
Served daily from 11am - 4pm
APPETIZERS
SOUPS & GREENS
ENTREES
SANDWICHES
www.vicsontheriver.com

VIC'S
ON THE RIVER
RESTAURANT & BAR

VIC'S
ON THE RIVER
LUNCH
www.vicsontheriver.com

PICTURE
RECIPES MADE
WITH YOU
IN MIND
VIC'S
www.vicsontheriver.com

One&Only The Palm is an exclusive resort on Dubai's Palm Island and takes its influence from Andalusian architecture. North55 worked in close partnership with the interior designers to develop a range of restuarant collateral that reflected the beautiful patterns found within the resort.

For the in-room directory we moved away from the traditional leather folder and developed a unique ring-bound trio of directories with foiled floral motifs. The lobby lounge menus were designed using sumptuous soft paper with foil and embossed patterns to compliment the exquisite surroundings.

The set of seven ZEST menus were designed to be clean and simple to allow for frequent updating. The colour palette was devised to stand out within the light and airy conservatory-style setting and to enable waiting staff to easily identify the different menus by.

One&Only The Palm

Design Agency: North55
Designer: Craig Falconer
Client: One&Only Resorts

One&Only Spa
In-Room Dining
Welcome

ZEST

ZEST

Urbano is a casual Italian restaurant within the Dubai's popular Downtown area.

The brand identity juxtaposes 1950s-style typography with modern-day urban Italian imagery to both reflect the restaurant's culinary heritage and create a contemporary look and feel, while also establishing an instantly recognisable visual language, personality and vibrancy. The restrained graphic colour palette was inspired by traditional olive tones found throughout Italy.

Urbano

Design Agency: North55
Designer: Alison Owen / Craig Falconer
Client: Jumeirah Group, Dubai

Urbano
Urbano
Urbano

Urbano
Urbano
Urbano

أوربانو
Urbano

Urbano
Urbano
ANTIPASTI Appetizers
A selection of antipasti from the counter
S 40.00 M 60.00
Caprese con bufala
Tomatoes with buffalo mozzarella and basil 45.00
Arancini rustici
Mozzarella fritta
Bresaola alla citronella
Bruschetta al pomodoro e basilico
LE PASTE E RISOTTI
Pasta & Risotto
Spaghetti aglio olio e peperoncino S 22.00 M 32.00
Spaghetti with chilli, garlic and oil
Penne all'arrabbiata
Penne with tomato and anchovy sauce
Paccheri con broccoli e gamberi
Risotto al battuto di mare
Urbano
LE PIZZE Pizza
Marinara
Margherita

Urbano

ANTIPASTI Appetizers
A selection of antipasti from the counter S 40.00 M 60.00
Caprese con bufala 45.00
Tomatoes with buffalo mozzarella and basil
Arancini rustici 30.00
Mozzarella fritta 34.00
Bresaola alla citronella 40.00
Bruschetta al pomodoro e basilico 28.00
Tomato and basil bruschetta
LE PASTE E RISOTTI Pasta & Risotto
Spaghetti aglio olio e peperoncino S 22.00 M 32.00
Penne all'arrabbiata S 25.00 M 35.00
Paccheri con broccoli e gamberi S 36.00 M 58.00
Risotto al battuto di mare S 40.00 M 65.00
Spaghetti alla chitarra allo scoglio 68.00
Spaghetti alle vongole S 35.00 M 52.00
Spaghetti with clams
Gnocchi al ragù d'anatra S 40.00 M 65.00
Urbano
LE PIZZE Pizza
Marinara 38.00
Margherita 45.00
Ai frutti di mare - Seafood 50.00
Quattro formaggi - Four cheeses 47.00
Alle verdure - Grilled vegetables 55.00
Alla valdostana 55.00
Ai gamberetti 48.00
Alla crudaiola 54.00
Al gorgonzola e rucola 48.00
Alla Napoletana 55.00
Capricciosa all'uovo 50.00
Sorriso 75.00
Rockefeller 75.00
Fiorentina 48.00
Additional toppings 5.00
DOLCI Desserts
Tiramisù 30.00
Bunet 30.00
Chocolate and amaretti baked custard
Pannacotta ai frutti di bosco 30.00
Mangia e bevi 30.00
Mousse di mascarpone e cioccolato bianco al caramello 30.00
Torta di pere al cioccolato caldo 30.00
Fondente al cioccolato con amarena 30.00
Selezione di gelati 25.00
Selection of ice cream
ALL PRICES SUBJECT TO 10% SERVICE CHARGE
Urbano
Urbano
Urbano
Urbano

Named for its flamboyant owner, Roberto's colourful identity was designed to reflect this lively Italian restaurant's lively character, and to help it stand out in Dubai's highly competitive financial district.

Roberto's

Design Agency: North55
Designer: Kelly Cartwright
Client: Roberto's Dubai

Roberto Rella
Managing Partner
Roberto's

Roberto Rella
Managing Partner
Roberto's

Rosalind Roongseang collaborated with Jin Thai Cuisine Restaurant to create a new identity that was Thai-inspired as well as modern. The challenge was to fuse the two worlds and be able to stand out from the numerous competitors in Chicago, Illinois. The use of the classic Thai pattern became an integral part of the branding that coexists with the modern interior design of the restaurant. The menus, signage, and carry out materials use vibrant colors to reflect the bold flavors of the Southeast Asian dishes which have made this tiny restaurant a big neighborhood hit.

Rosalind Roongseang's broad range of experience in design allows her to work across the board, whether it's a branding, packaging, or a web design project. She is able to solve design problems from conceptual stage to realization and is currently working and living in New York City, NY.

Jin Thai Restaurant

Designer: Rosalind Roongseang

JIN
JIN
JIN

Launched in San Francisco with plans for broad expansion, Roam Artisan Burgers brings sustainability to the traditional burger joint. They work only with local purveyors providing a natural diet and habitat for their beef, turkey and buffalo. They offer nutritionally appropriate portions and ingredients. The challenge was to convey that message in a pervasive, but not heavy-handed way. They don't want to lecture customers, but want to differentiate themselves in a market clogged with competition. All materials used in the construction, signage and printed collateral are sustainable, reclaimed and appropriate to the integrity of the brand.

Roam Artisan Burgers

Design Agency: Rubber Design

SAN
OAM
BURGERS
HOUSE-MADE
VEGGIE
FREE-RANGE
TURKEY
GRASS-FED
BEEF
ALL-NATURAL
BISON

FREE-RANGE
TURKEY

ARTISAN
ROAM
BURGERS

Sauce is Chef Frank Prisinzano's 4th East Village (NYC) restaurant joining Frank, Lil Frankies and Supper. And following in the footsteps of Franks other restaurants, Sauce is warm, authentic, with an almost undersigned design esthetic. The food is minimalist Italian cuisine with Ragu as a focal point. But, different than the others, Sauce is also a butcher and grocery. The sign itself was inspired by old New York pork store and Italian grocery storefronts, where sometimes it feels like information overload. Our storefront sign takes that idea, but gives it a more modern spin.

Sauce Restaurant

Design Agency: Meter Industries
Creative Director: Marty Weiss
Designer: Andrea D'Aquino, Eulie Lee

Sauce
78-84 Rivington STREET
NEW YORK, NY 10002
212.420.7700
SAUCERESTAURANT.COM
Sauce
Sauce

Sauce
Sauce
Sauce

Sauce
MEATBALL HERO
Sauce
T-BONE

Sauce
Sauce

Sauce
Sauce
Sauce
Sauce
Sauce
Sauce
Sauce

Sauce
FUSILLI MARINARA

Sauce
Sauce
Sauce
Sauce
Sauce

Sauce
Sauce
Sauce
Sauce

SAUSAGES
SAUCES

TUTTO LA NOSTRA PRODUZIONE
Sauce
EVERYTHING MADE BY US
ANTIPASTI
Crostino del giorno $4.95
Fried zucchini match sticks $4.95
Raw fennel "oysters" & black salt $4.95
Roasted peppers with Bagna Caoda $4.95
Zucchini tagliatelle and Bottarga $6.95
Stuffed Pepper with farro & sausage $6.95
Rare Roast Beef with virgin oil, arugula & coarse grey salt $6.95
FAMILY STYLE FEASTS
For 4 or more only. Priced per person
NEO-ragu Cencione with gravy, platter of meatballs, sausages & braciole and Arugula salad $14.95 PP
BIG BOLOGNA Pappardelle with Grass Fed bolognese, any 2 contorni and Arugula salad $16.95 PP
THE POMODORO Spaghetti Alla Chitarra with passato and Arugula salad $10.95 PP
VERONESE Polenta & gorgonzola, sausages and Arugula salad $13.95 PP
WELCOME TO THE old world. WE HAND PICK ALL OF OUR PRODUCTS. WE KNOW all of our suppliers.
CASH ONLY
HOUSE SPECIALTIES
"THE PLANK" (2 or more) Soft Polenta on wood with Grass Fed bolognese $8.95 PP
"ICE BOX" FUSILLI Marinara, soft ricotta cheese, pecorino & oreganata breadcrumbs $7.95
add Our Sausage $3.95
BAKED FARRO MACARONI crusty and chewy $7.95
add Grass Fed meatballs $3.95
POTATO LINGUINE Brown butter, fried sage, coarse grey salt & a crispy pastured egg $7.95
LASAGNA ALLA BOLOGNESE Grass Fed bolognese, besciamella $7.95
"BOBO BRODO" Meat tortelloni in brodo with greens and meatballs $9.95
add a perfect pastured egg $2.95
VERONESE Sausage, polenta, gorgonzola dolce $9.95
NOSE TO TAIL MEATS
BOLLITO MISTO (slowly braised, sliced meats) Grass Fed Beef & Heritage Pork Served with salsa Verde, salsa Rosso & Mostarda di frutta di Cremona $14.95
ARROSTO MISTO (roasted meats) Grass Fed Beef, Heritage Pork and Turkey Served with sugo d'Arrosto & roasted tomato $14.95
PASTURED HERITAGE CHICKEN Served with funghi (mixed mushroom gravy)
Leg $8.95
Breast $10.95
"TAGLIATA" Sliced Tuscan Style Steak over arugula salad with shaved parmigiano cheese & sliced tomato (priced daily)
"SERGIO LEONE" Steak Alla Pizzaiola with crispy pastured egg & broccoli rabe $14.95
"THE STEAK HOUSE" For 2 or 4. Served with four contorni of your choice MP
CONTORNI
Soft Parmigiano Polenta $4.95
Mashed Potatoes and basil oil $3.95
Yams with butter and sage $3.95
Beets and berries $3.95
Slow roasted Fennel $4.95
Roasted Rosemary potatoes $4.95
Green beans cooked in passato $3.95
Butter glazed carrots $3.95
Broccoli rabe and toasted garlic $4.95
My roasted tomatoes $4.95
Sauce

TUTTO LA NOSTRA PRODUZIONE
EVERYTHING MADE BY US
Sauce
ABOUT
menu
GALLERY
BLOG
CONTACT
78-84 RIVINGSTON STREET
NEW YORK, NY 10002
FOR RESERVATION
212.420.7700
MON-SAT 11:30AM - 11PM
SUN NOON - 10:30PM
VISIT OUR SISTER RESTAURANTS
FRANK LIL' FRANKIE'S SUPPER

Small identity for one of Norway finest restaurants Renaa Restauranter, the restaurant is build around the norwegian top chef Sven Erik Reena who has had great sucess and won numerous prizes for his cooking.

We went for a personal and clean scandinavian approach wich reflects the style of food he makes.

The concept is based on guests making a food journey. The basic values include concepts such as absolutely fresh, modern Norwegian and natural. The restaurant consists of two areas, a dining room (Renaa Restauranten) and a food bar (Renaa Matbaren), both of which maintain top-quality level but which offer different settings and expressions. Combining the two areas we get Renaa Restaurants.

Identity for Renaa Restauranter

Designer: Runar Lillegård

A restaurant identity encompassing logo, menu, bag and assorted supporting materials. The restaurant concept is taking everything you loved (or hated) about middle school and repurposing it for adults. Hence, drinks with names like The Homecoming Queen, The Burnout and The Teacher's Pet. You'll find menu items arranged by school subject and a decidedly adult approach to the lunch tray and milk cartons.

Homeroom

Designer: Susannah Briggs

Homeroom
Your Afterschool Happy Hour
Rachel's breath shines!
J+R
Kayla and Amy
BFFS 4 Eva!
Homeroom
Your Afterschool Happy Hour
K+A
Mike has cooties!
Bobby and Jessie,
Sittin' in a tree.
K-I-S-S-I-N-G!
Miss Woodall
Smells like an
old goat!
Boys are gross!
Homeroom
Your Afterschool Happy Hour
Pink Pearl
Mr. Thompson's
a dirty old man!
Alex smells
like butt!

Chemistry

{Booze}

Gin & juicebox
Hendricks gin and Berry Juicy Juice
"Who packed YOUR lunch?"
7

Mrs. Crabapple's Midday Snack
Vodka, pink lemonade
No wonder she's so cheerful...
7

Homecoming Queen
White wine spritzer, hunger pangs
7

The Mathlete
Coffee, Jim Beam, Quadratic Equations, wedgie
6

The Cheerleader
Sweet Tea vodka, Lemonade, Plan B
7

Honors Student
Redbull, vodka, served with caffeine pill and cigarette
Acing the test was never more fun
8

Head Coach
Tallboy of Pabst, shot of Jim Beam, restraining order
7

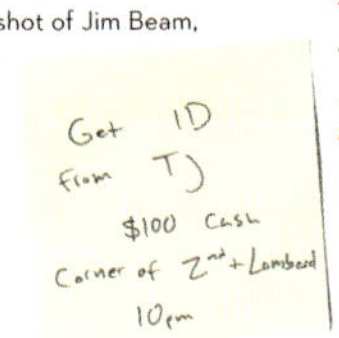

Locker-Room Punch
Koolaid (Cherry or Strawberry) and coconut rum
Served with a choice of towel-snapping, depantsing, noogies, or a swirlie
7

Mr. Thornton's Locked Desk Drawer
Shot of Jack, side of self-loathing
3

Miss Popular
Peach schnapps, 7-Up
Best served under the bleachers at the Home Game
7

The Burnout
40 oz Olde English in a paper bag behind the school
3

The Naive Girl
Long Island Iced Tea
"This iced tea tastes kinda funny..."
8

The Jock
Bottle of Bud Light and a shot of Old Crow
"Gonna get waaasted, man"
5

Teacher's Pet
Appletini and the hatred of your peers
8

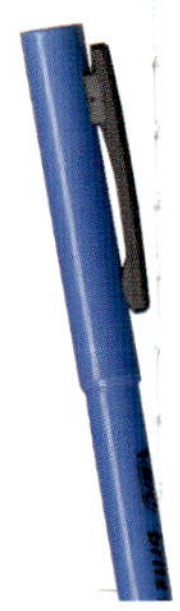

Botany

{Salads & Other Green Things}

Malus domestica et Arachis hypogaea
(Apples, homemade peanut butter, and local honey)
5

Lactuca sativa Caesar viridis
(Caesar Salad with croutons and anchovies)
8

Lactuca beta vulgaris
(Local lettuce, roasted beets, blue cheese, orange-fennel vinaigrette)
9

Lactuca beta vulgaris
(Local lettuce, roasted beets, blue cheese, orange-fennel vinaigrette)
9

Eruca sativa salad
(Arugula salad with warm goat cheese, candied fruit and lentils)
8

Tuber aestivum illinoinensis
(Baby farm leaves & herbs, black truffle vinaigrette and pecan picada)
9

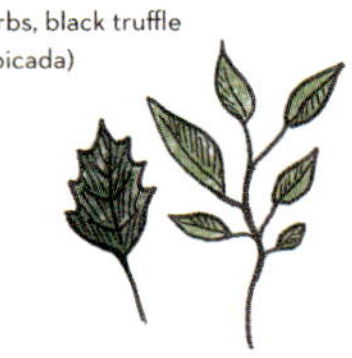

Spanish Class

{Mexican Food}

Moctezuma's Last Stand
Cheese or Chicken Chile Rellenos topped with guacamole and served with a side of bloody sacrifice.
"Blessed by the solar emperor Offer expires December 21, 2012"
17

Soporte Pasado de Moctezuma
El queso o el pollo Chile Rellenos remató con guacamole y sirvió con un lado del sacrificio sangriento.
"Bendecido por el emperador solar La oferta expira el 21 de diciembre de 2012"
17

Zapatista Nachos
Fightin' corn chips with guacamole, chipotle cheese, black olives, sour cream, scallions and mango-corn salsa
Served with a side of bloody revolución!
16 Add a grilled socialist chicken for 18

Nachos de Zapatista
Virutas de maíz de Fightin con guacamole, queso del chipotle, las aceitunas negras, la crema amarga, scallions y salsa del mango-maíz
¡Servido con un lado del revolución sangriento!
16 *Agregue un pollo socialista asado a la parilla para* 18

American History

{Home Cookin'}

Dirty Jersey Chicken nuggets
With honey mustard and BBQ Sauce
Served with a side of greasy guido and has been known to cause quite the Situation
9

The Happiest Meal
Free-range organic burger with choice of soft drink, apple juice or milk and curly fries or apples and honey
Lovin' it since June 1979
22 Add cheese and onions for 24

Fried Chicken Supper
Served with mashed potatoes, gravy, collards and bacon and a sourdough biscuit
Down-home cookin' jus' like Ma used to make! Served only to REAL 'Mericans. You betcha!
20

Sloppy Joes
Free-range beef, caramelized onions, ketchup and a side of coleslaw
Truly a great American invention: soiling shirts since 1987
17

Latin

{Italian Food}

Mussolini's mini pizze quadrate
A heady combination of Nationalist heirloom pomodoro, fresh mozzarella and basil
Il Duce's favorite wild funghi, roasted garlic, and grilled pollo
Side of Fascism not required, police state recommended
10

M. Lisa's Maccheroni e Formaggio
Baked with breadcrumbs
Da Vinci himself would call this a masterpiece!
15 Add tartufi, onions, enigmatic smiles, grilled pollo or rabe del broccolo for 17

Home Ec

{Dessert}

Halloween Candy Stash
May include mini Snickers, Milky Way, Reese's Cups, Tootsie Pops, and Chocolate Kisses
"Hey kid... want some candy?"
7

Mr. Bulleit's Inappropriate Remarks
Vanilla ice cream, caramel and shot of Bulleit bourbon
"You'll do anything to get an A...?"
12

Orange You Glad School's Out?
Orange vodka, orange juice, vanilla ice cream
12

Mrs. Woodall Splits School
Banana, butterscotch schnapps, vanilla ice cream, chocolate syrup, sprinkles
15

Three Oreos and a White Russian
The Dude would be proud
6

Cotton Candy Pom-Poms
Served with a side of Jailbait for a one 5-year prison sentence
7

Mrs. Lamberth's Strawberry Surprise
Strawberry ice cream, strawberry schnapps, whipped cream, maraschino cherry
12

Go TEAM! Root Float
ROOT liqueur (tastes like root beer!), vanilla ice cream
"The alcoholic childhood you never had"
15

... What was her name, again?
Jessica? Jaime? ... Shit.

Call Me
215-439-5126

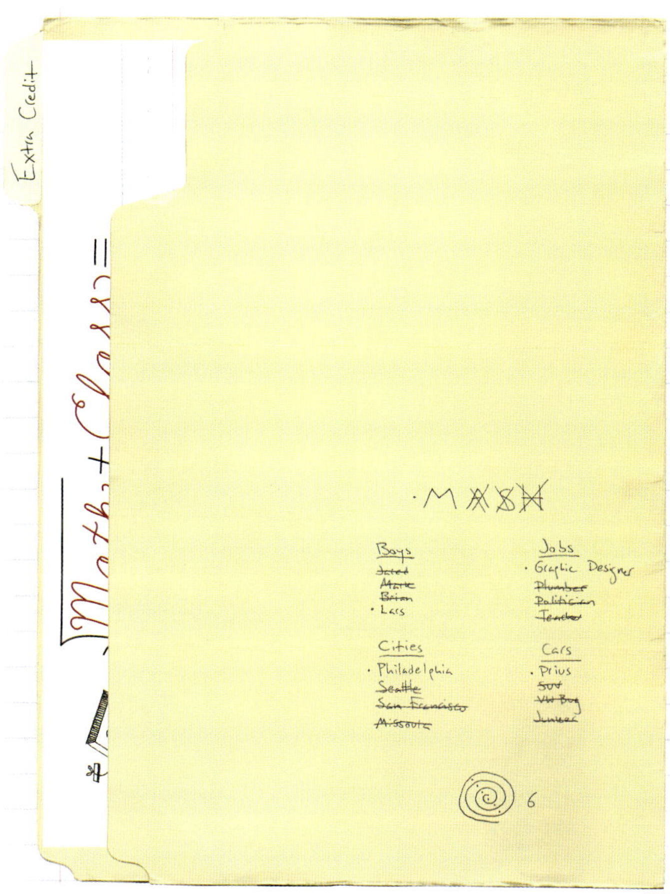

Useful Information

Dad keeps his booze in the garage in a box labeled "Happy family memories"

MULTIPLICATION TABLE

1	2	3	4	5	6	7	8	9	10	11	12
2	4	6	8	10	12	14	16	18	20	22	24
3	6	9	12	15	18	21	24	27	30	33	36
4	8	12	16	20	24	28	32	36	40	44	48
5	10	15	20	25	30	35	40	45	50	55	60
6	12	18	24	30	36	42	48	54	60	66	72
7	14	21	28	35	42	49	56	63	70	77	84
8	16	24	32	40	48	56	64	72	80	88	96
9	18	27	36	45	54	63	72	81	90	99	108
10	20	30	40	50	60	70	80	90	100	110	120
11	22	33	44	55	66	77	88	99	110	121	132
12	24	36	48	60	72	84	96	108	120	132	144

Average price of Plan B: $25

Table of Time Measure

60 seconds = 1 minute
60 minutes = 1 hour
24 hours = 1 day
7 days = 1 week
30 days = 1 calendar month
12 months = 1 year
365 days = 1 common year
366 days = 1 leap year
100 years = 1 century

Table of Dry Measure

2 pints (pt.) = 1 quart (qt.)
8 quarts = 1 peck (pk.)
4 pecks = 1 bushel (bu.)
1 cord = 128 cu. ft.

Table of Liquid Measure

4 gills (gi.) = 1 pint (pt.)
2 pints = 1 quart (qt.)
4 quarts = 1 gallon (gal.)
31½ gallons = 1 barrel (bbl.)
2 barrels = hogshead (hhd.)

Table of Paper Measure

24 sheets = 1 quire
20 quires = 1 ream
10 reams = 1 bale

Table of Linear Measure

12 inches = 1 foot
3 feet = 1 yard
16½ ft. (5½ yds.) = 1 rod
660 feet = 1 furlong
320 rods (5280 ft.) = 1 mile

Miscellaneous Measures

12 units = 1 dozen
12 doz. = 1 gross
12 gr. = 1 great gross
20 units = 1 score
1 hand = 4 inches
1 fathom = 6 feet
1 knot = 6086 feet
3 knots = 1 league
1 bu. potatoes = 60 lbs.
1 barrel flour = 196 lbs.
1 cu. ft. of water = 7.48 liquid gals. and weighs. 62.425 lbs.
Diameter of circle x 3.1416 = circumference
Diameter of circle squared x .7854 = area.
Atmospheric pressure is 14.7 lbs. per sq. in. at sea level.
13½ cu. ft. of air weighs 1 lb.

Table of Cubic Measure

1728 cubic inches = 1 cubic foot
27 cubic feet = 1 cubic yard
128 cubic feet = 1 cord of wood
24¾ cubic feet = 1 perch of stone

NOTE – A cord of wood is a pile 8 feet long, 4 feet wide and 4 feet high. A perch of stone or brick is 16½ feet long, 1½ feet wide, and 1 foot high.

Table of Avoirdupois Weight

16 drams = 1 ounce (oz.)
16 ounces = 1 pound (lb.)
100 pounds = 1 hundredweight (cwt.)
2000 pounds = 1 ton (T.)
2240 pounds = 1 long ton (L. T.)

Table of Troy Weight

24 grains (gr.) = 1 pennyweight (dwt.)
20 pennyweights = 1 ounce (oz.)
12 ounces = 1 pound (lb.)

Table of Circular Measure

60 seconds (") = 1 minute (')
60 minutes = 1 degree (°)
360 degrees = 1 circumference
A degree of the earth's surface or a meridian = 69.16 miles at the equator,

Table of Apothecaries' Weight

20 grains (gr.) = 1 scruple (℈)
3 scruples = 1 dram (ʒ)
8 drams = 1 ounce (℥)
12 ounces = 1 pound (lb.)

Table of Surface Measure

144 sq. in. = 1 sq. ft.
9 sq. ft. = 1 sq. yd.
30¼ sq. yds. = 1 sq. rod
160 sq. rods = 1 acre
640 acres = 1 sq. mile
An acre measures 208.71 ft. on each side.
A section of land is 1 sq. mile.
A quarter section is 160 acres.
A township is 36 sq. miles.

Location of keys, wallet, dignity...?

CONVERSION TABLES

LENGTH
1 meter (m) = 100 cm = 1,000 mm
1 millimeter (mm) = .001 m
1 centimeter (cm) = .01 m
1 decimeter (dm) = .1 m
1 decameter (dkm) = 10 m
1 hectometer (hm) = 100 m
1 kilometer (km) = 1,000 m

CAPACITY
1 liter (l) = 100 cl = 1,000 ml
1 milliliter (ml) = .001 l
1 centiliter (cl) = .01 l
1 deciliter (dl) = .1 l
1 decaliter (dkl) = 10 l
1 hectoliter (hl) = 100 l
1 kiloliter (kl) = 1,000 l

Becky's # 215-531-2097

WEIGHT
1 gram (g) = 100 cg = 1,000 mg
1 milligram (mg) = .001 g
1 centigram (cg) = .01 g
1 decigram (dg) = .1 g
1 decagram (dkg) = 10 g
1 hectogram (hg) = 100 g
1 kilogram (kg) = 1,000 g

Ashley's # 215-483-6212

METERS	YARDS	INCHES
1.000	1.093	39.37
.914	1.000	36.00

CENTIMETERS	INCHES	FEET
1.00	.394	.0328
2.54	1.000	1/12
30.48	12.000	1.000

Door Code for teacher's lounge: 39475

GRAMS	OUNCES	POUNDS
1.00	.035	.002
28.35	1.000	1/16
453.59	16.000	1.000
1,000.00	35.274	2.205

KILOGRAMS	OUNCES	POUNDS
1.000	35.274	2.205
.028	1.000	1/16
.454	16.000	1.000

LITERS	PINTS	QUARTS	GAL.
1.000	2.113	1.057	.264
.473	1.000	1/2	1/8
.946	2.000	1.000	1/4
3.785	8.000	4.000	1.000

Brand restyling for the new chef José Andrés Jaleo restaurant at The Cosmopolitan Hotel Las Vegas specialized in Spanish cuisine. Design of the daily use materials and other graphic elements for the interior (wallpaper inspired a Mantilla and lettering for the main entrance doors and others). Interior design project developed by Rockwell and Rockwell Group Europe.

Jaleo Restaurant, Las Vegas

Design Agency: Toormix
Client: Think Food Group - Chef José Andrés
Interior Photos' Photographer: Jeff Green

JALEO
BY JOSÉ ANDRÉS

SPANISH LESSONS AT
JALEO
BY JOSÉ ANDRÉS
¡GRACIAS!
THANK YOU!
SPANISH LESSONS AT
JALEO
BY JOSÉ ANDRÉS
¡SALUD!
CHEERS!
SPANISH LESSONS AT
JALEO
BY JOSÉ ANDRÉS
¡BUEN PROVECHO!
ENJOY YOUR MEAL!
SPANISH LESSONS AT
JALEO
BY JOSÉ ANDRÉS
LA CUENTA POR FAVOR
CHECK PLEASE
SPANISH LESSONS AT
JALEO
BY JOSÉ ANDRÉS
¡UNA DE BRAVAS!
AN ORDER OF BRAVAS POTATOES!
SPANISH LESSONS AT
JALEO
BY JOSÉ ANDRÉS
ALGO PARA PICAR
SOMETHING TO SNACK ON

The latest restaurant design by Ralston & Bau is an intimate space in Paris that is dedicated to a balanced fusion of Japanese and French gastronomy. "Sous les Cerisiers" (under the cherry trees) is an invitation to taste the delicious cooking of Sakura.

Both cultures have influenced the theatrical interior concept. The classic opera and geisha cultures from France and Japan can be seen in the scenographic layers, costumes and shadows cast throughout the interior. A contrast of dark and light spaces divides the room: the bright area with the bar as a center point is used for cooking courses during the daytime, and the dark part, following a perspective angle, including a VIP space to enjoy a gastronomic menu at night.

Moveable and translucent walls separate the seating areas for privacy.

The theatrical influence from the interior design is continued in the development of the visual identity of the "Sous les Cerisiers" restaurant. A traditional textile costume clasp with soft, natural curves was the inspiration for the logo. The menu cards soft golden paper follows up the costume idea: through pre-punched holes a delicate ribbon bound the changeable menu sheets inside. Each menu uses a different style of classical theatre costume ribbon.

The official launch of the restaurant took place the 22 of September 2009.

Sous les Cerisiers

Design Agency: Transplant
Mission: Japanese-french Restaurant
Client: Sakura Franck

La Carte des vins
& boissons
Sous Les Cerisiers
Restaurant
12 rue Stanislas, Paris 6e
Atelier
Cours de cuisine

La Carte du restaurant

La Carte des vins
& boissons

La Carte des vins
& boissons
Sous les Cerisiers

The River restaurant didn't just want a strong opening night, they were aiming at becoming an iconic restaurant for our town, so I was invited in as a designer to build an image for them that showed strength and refinement. Starting with the custom stainless steel logo, it would be the first thing customers see. I contrasted the very dark furniture with light curtains and tablecloths, immersed in a warm light. This created an inviting environment that patrons could see through the glass wall as they drove by. Even the table disposition was given a lot of thought, as well as the materials in construction and lighting, down to the uniforms of the employees. River has been open for 2 years now and remains a successful venture.

RIVER
RESTAURANTE

River Restaurant

Designer: Rui Dias / treh5.com
3D Designer: Ruben Neves
Client: River Restaurante
Photographer: Rui Dias

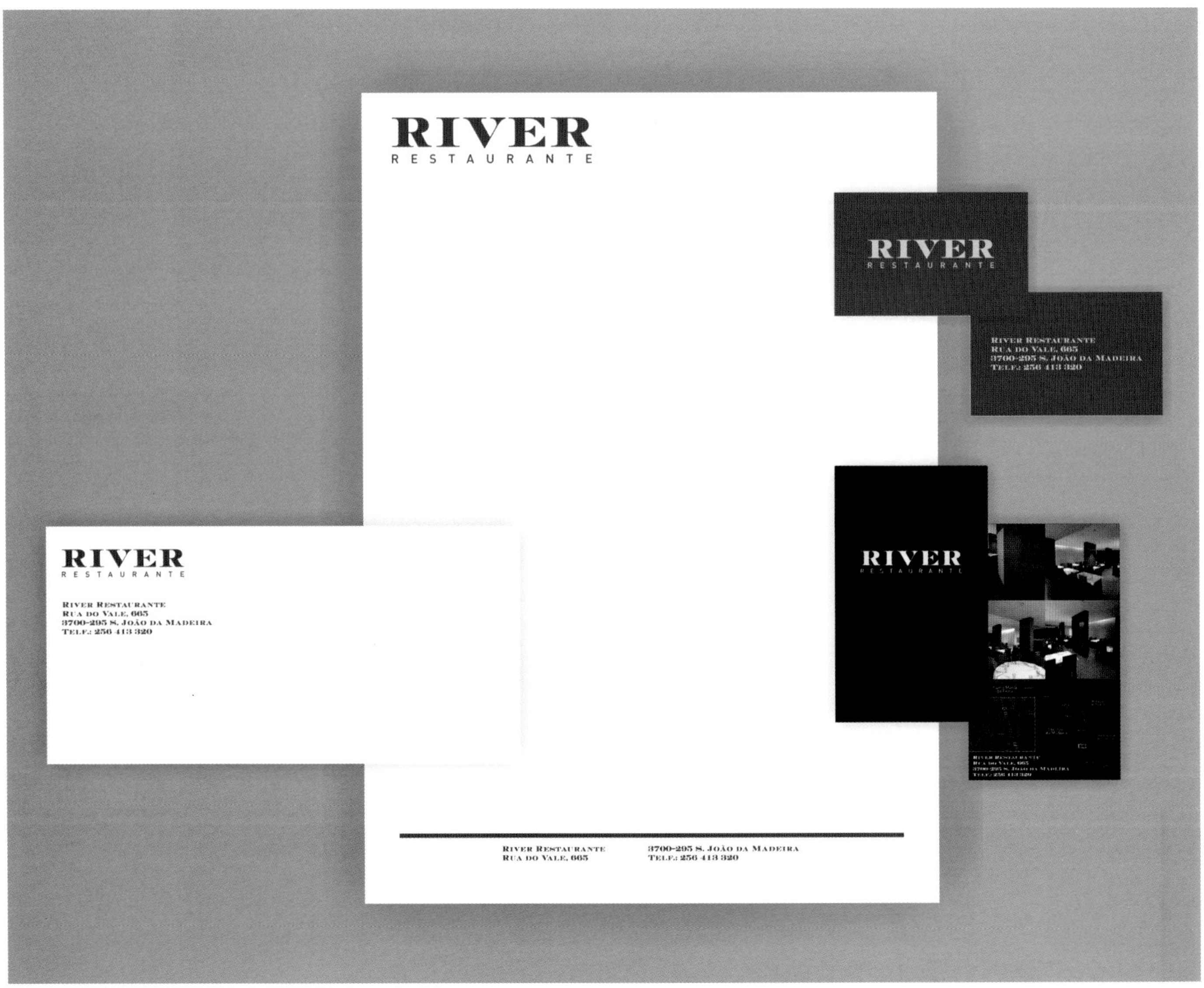

RIVER

UXUS was approached by a leading restaurateur in California to create a unique dining concept for their new location in California's State Capital, Sacramento. UXUS created a complete restaurant concept including the interior restaurant layout and design as well as the branding and house style.

The restaurant covers an area of 700 m^2 and seats 250 guests. All areas of the restaurant - bar, wine cellar, main dining area & private dining - were created by UXUS.

Central to Ella's concept is the communal dining experience of the Table d'Hôte, which is designed to make the diners feel as if the chef has invited them to a private dinner party in his kitchen.

Ella has won many international design awards and has been featured on the cover of several major design publications.

Ella Dining Room & Bar

Design Agency: UXUS
Designers/Architects: UXUS
Creative Director: George Gottl & Oliver Michell
Client: The Selzim Restaurant Group
Photographer: M. Wessing

thank you!

DINING ROOM ella BAR

DINING ROOM ella BAR

The Kitchen
ella
SELLAND'S
The Kitchen Restaurant
Ella Dining Room & Bar
Selland's Market-Café

DINING ROOM ella BAR

DINING ROOM ella BAR

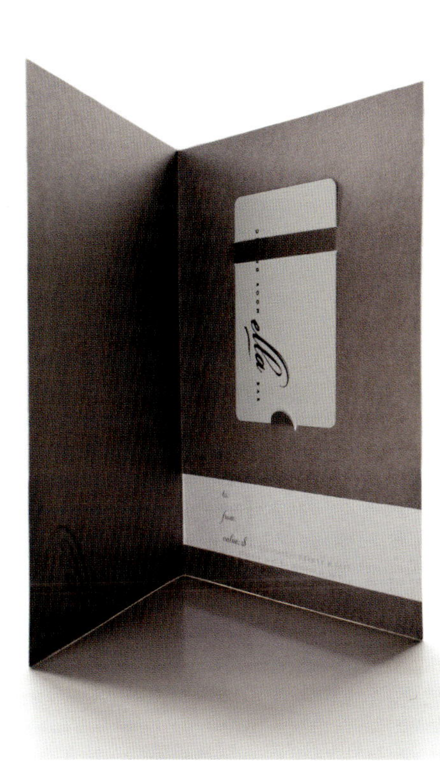

DINING ROOM ella BAR
DINING ROOM ella BAR

Wandrahm is a quality restaurant located in the new famous district of Hamburg called "Hafencity".

Wandrahm

Design Agency: Vingervlug
Interior Design: Oliver Widmann
Logo Design: Kira Peters
Photographer: Vingervlug / Markus Voigt

WANDRAHM
RESTAURANT & BAR

WANDRAHM
COFFEE & TEA

WANDRAHM
COFFEE & TEA

Na Strelaku means 'to the polygon'. This restaurant is located in a park which was hosting a polygon facility during the 9th Century. The quietness and the history embed in these premises, close to the Austrian borders, inspired ideas of slow living and food appreciation.

Main concepts are indeed the conviviality, the joy of sharing and a new interpretation of Rococo' style.

Na Strelaku Restaurant

Designer: Viviane Mosso

simplicity
tradition
elegance
virtue
actions/gestures
joy of conviviality
slow living
historical heritage
surroundings
vegetarian choice
gluttony

Autumn
menu
A bit of History
Na Strelaku means 'to the polygon'.
This restaurant is located in a park which was hosting a polygon facility during the 9th Century. The quietness and the history embed in these premises, inspired an idea of slow living and food appreciation.
Main concepts are indeed the conviviality, the joy of sharing and a new interpretation of Rococo' style.
Restaurace
Na Střeláku
Restaurace
Na Střeláku

Menu
Wine list
Menu
Starters
Smoked salmon gateau
Baked figs & goat's cheese
Roasted Figs with Goat Cheese
Simple and delicious gourmet
Mains
Grilled sirloin steak
walnuts and blue

RESTAURACE
NA STŘELÁKU

Restaurace Na Strelaku
RESTAURACE NA STŘELÁKU

NA STŘ
RESTAU
Na Str
RESTAURACE
NA STŘELAKU

Restaurace Na Strelaku

Leandro Estevam is an art director that decided to open a Japanese restaurant, the first of this kind in Catanduva, São Paulo. He first contacted me to illustrate a wall on the sushi bar. But after talking about the project, we both decided to create a complete visual identity for the place, with guerrilla advertising, ads, illustrations, among other items. The challenge was to create something unique, modern, but elegant as well.

We chose a palette that combined red, black, white and gold, with modern vector illustrations.

It was used a lot of patterns in this project, pop elements from Japanese culture, along with a simple serif font. Since the illustration was already very appealing, we picked a clean font to balance the layout.

For the texts, which were created by copywriter Fernando Cabral, we used humor, creating titles such as "Japan has invaded the city. And used it's most powerful weapon: Culinary." Another fun piece is a guerrilla advertising using stickers in cars, making the impression that a ninja star had stricken the window. The sticker was perfectly removable, without leaving any marks.

The final result of the visual identity is something fun, pop, but also very charming and captivating, making people curious about the restaurant and willing to get to know it.

Hai Sushi Bar

Designer: Carol Rivello and Leandro Estevam
Client: Leandro Estevam
Location: São Paulo
Photographer: La Luce, Leandro Estevam, Carol Rivello

夢
神
愛
禅

夢
愛
神
禅

BILLBOARD
O Japão vai dominar
CATANDUVA.
AGUARDE!

PATTERNS

PAPER TRAY
PLATE
NAPKIN
Hai
SUSHI BAR

AD
O JAPÃO INVADIU A CIDADE.
E USOU A SUA ARMA MAIS
PODEROSA: A CULINÁRIA.
CHEGOU HAI, O PRIMEIRO SUSHI BAR DE CATANDUVA.
Hai
SUSHI.BAR

TAKE OUT OPTIONS

UNIFORMS

STICKERS
LETTERHEAD
BUSINESS CARDS
PINS

SUSHI BAR
OHAI AMBIENTES CARDÁPIO NOVIDADES LOCALIZAÇÃO CONTATO
Requinte e tradição, no primeiro sushi bar DE CATANDUVA.
Ambientes
Conheça os ambientes **elegantes** e aconchegantes do nosso espaço. Lor em Ipsum.
leia mais +
Cardápio
O Restaurante Hai possui um menu **surpreendente** com combinações que você vai adorar.
leia mais +
Newsletter
Deseja receber informações sobre promoções, sorteios, novidades no cardápio hai? Faça parte da nossa **newsletter!**
Digite seu e-mail »
ok
Siga o Hai »
INICIAL OHAI AMBIENTES CARDÁPIO NOVIDADES LOCALIZAÇÃO CONTATO

Hai SUSHI BAR
OHAI
AMBIENTES
CARDÁPIO
NOVIDADES
LOCALIZAÇÃO
CONTATO
Conheça o Restaurante
Lorem Ipsum is simply dummy text of the printing and typesetting industry. Lorem Ipsum has been the industry's standard dummy text ever since the 1500s, when an unknown printer took a galley of type and scrambled it to make a type specimen book. It has survived not only five
centuries, but also the leap into electronic typesetting, remaining essentially unchanged. It was popularised in the 1960s with the release of Letraset sheets containing Lorem Ipsum passages, and more recently with desktop publishing software like Aldus PageMaker.
Proposta Hai
Lorem Ipsum is simply dummy text of the printing and typesetting industry. Lorem Ipsum has been the industry's standard dummy text ever since the 1500s, when an unknown printer took a galley of type and scrambled it to make a type specime
Nosso Conceito
Lorem Ipsum is simply dummy text of the printing and typesetting industry. Lorem Ipsum has been the industry's standard dummy text ever since the 1500s, when an unknown printer took a galley of type and scrambled it to make a type specime.
Ambientes
Conheça os ambientes elegantes e aconchegantes do nosso espaço. Lor em Ipsum.
leia mais +
Siga o Hai »
INICIAL
OHAI
AMBIENTES
CARDÁPIO
NOVIDADES
LOCALIZAÇÃO
CONTATO

日本

DDCA were responsible for re-launching The Majestic Hotel and creating a brand new Italian Restaurant in the Lake District, Francescas. We offered a range of services to the client including Branding, Design, Interior Design, Signage, Advertising, Copywriting, Art Direction & Photography, PR and a Marketing Campaign across all mediums.

"The logo and visual identity design had to reflect a traditional Italian restaurant. To carry the rustic aesthetic we introduced a bespoke hand drawn logotype in a hand painted style. This was carried throughout the brands collateral." Nick Johnson, Creative Director

DDCA designed and printed the evening and daytime menus for Francescas. Using photographs of the italian chefs and hand drawn illustrations of the authentic ingredients. The covers of the menus were printed using embossed leather to give a tactile and upmarket feel.

The Francescas Restaurant

Design Agency: Danielle Dunn Creative Agency

Francescas

RESTAURANT & PIZZERIA

WELCOME TO FRANCESCAS

A warm and friendly welcome to Francescas! We're passionate about good food and wine served in a vibrant Italian environment. If you're relaxing or celebrating you can feel at home, enjoy a great selection of dishes and great service!

Our menu is authentic and simple, cooked with love and passion using the best traditional and freshest ingredients. Our stone baked oven gives our pizza the true taste of Italy.

Check out our 'Specials Board' for seasonal, locally sourced dishes of the day, we hope you'll enjoy dining with us!

Buon Appetito

NELSON, PEDRO AND FRANCO

Nelson Pedro Franco

Love Food, Love Francescas

Exclusive Places is a project bringing together the most exclusive hotels, clubs and restaurants from Europe, all of them carefully selected by Exclusive Places Group connoisseurs, therefore its identity and design had to comply with certain requirements of such refined presentation.

The Exclusive Places logotype was designed in order to show the prestige and the actual exclusiveness of the brand, which leads a rigorous selection of units portrayed on the site. Simple white and black colours show the classic style of the project and the applied font reflects the opulence, wealth and uniqueness. The crown in the logotype is presented in a form of an outline - not to be overwhelming but classical, with three decorative points at the top - symbolizing crown jewels; additionally, the points along with the continuation resemble a sceptre. The crown mounted on the inscription symbolises the legitimate luxury trendsetter, a guide in the world of exclusiveness. As for the communication the logotype shows sophistication, elegance and high standards, all in order to build a sense of certainty and confidence of the brand.

Due to the extensive amount of content presented on the website, its layout has been maximally simplified as not to interfere with the information. The layout should not be overpowering - it was designed to create a background for the content presentation, hence the applied dark colour - while browsing the website the user will not be distracted. The layout is toned down, calm, here and there a golden colour emphasize its exclusiveness. In addition, black and golden colours perfectly reflect the concept of luxury found in the mission of Exclusive Places and subtly highlight the prestige of each presented place. The project, contrary to appearances, is characterised by minimalism - the logo and the website itself are rich, but not excessively overloaded.

Exclusive Places

Designer: Filip Kokoszynski
Client: Exclusive Places Group
Location: Poland

Exclusive Places
WWW.EXCLUSIVE-PLACES.COM
www.exclusive-places.com
group@exclusive-places.com
+48 792 628 171

pawel.skrzypczak@exclusive-places.com
area manager / Poland
+48 792 628 171
Exclusive Places

Exclusive Places
WWW.EXCLUSIVE-PLACES.COM

Exclusive Places
WWW.EXCLUSIVE-PLACES.COM

Exclusive Places
WWW.EXCLUSIVE-PLACES.COM
Hotels, restaurants, clubs // Poland

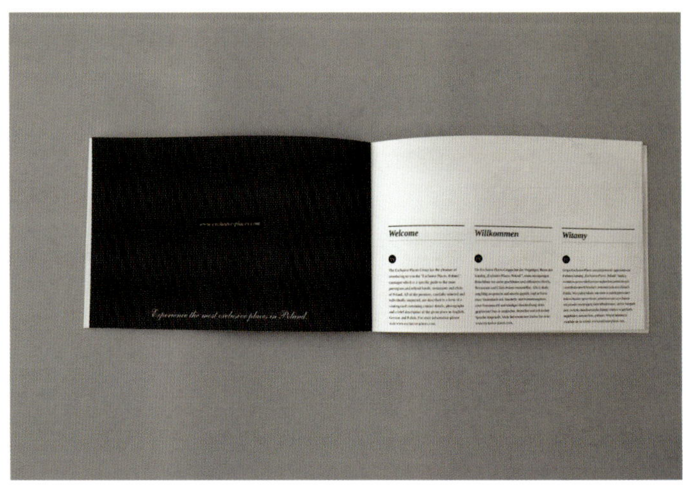
Welcome
Willkommen
Witamy

Experience
the most exclusive places in Europe

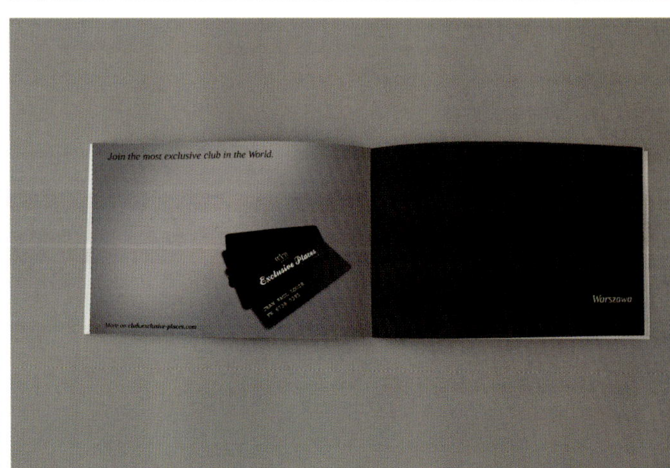
Join the most exclusive club in the World.
Warszawa

Exclusive Places
EXPERIENCE
THE
MOST
EXCLUSIVE
PLACES
IN
EUROPE
WWW.EXCLUSIVE-PLACES.COM

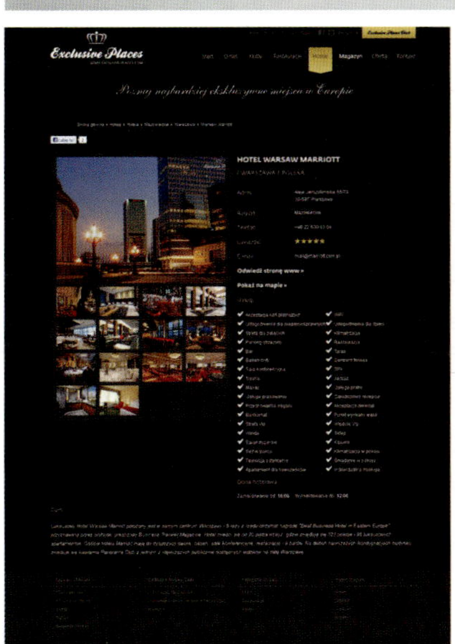
Exclusive Places
HOTEL WARSAW MARRIOTT

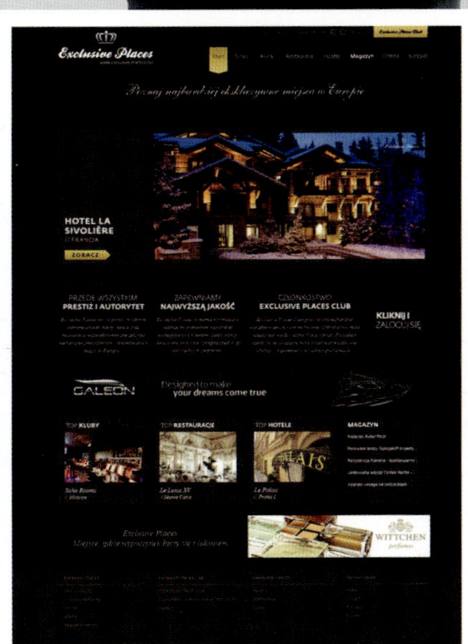
Exclusive Places
HOTEL LA SIVOLIÈRE

Exclusive Places

Brand and identity work for Sielankowo, a restaurant & hotel based in the Polish country side of famour, Mazury. The project involved logo generation, stationery, booklet and website.

Sielankowo Identity

Designer: Mateusz Piekarski
Client: Sielankowo
Location: Warszawa, Poland

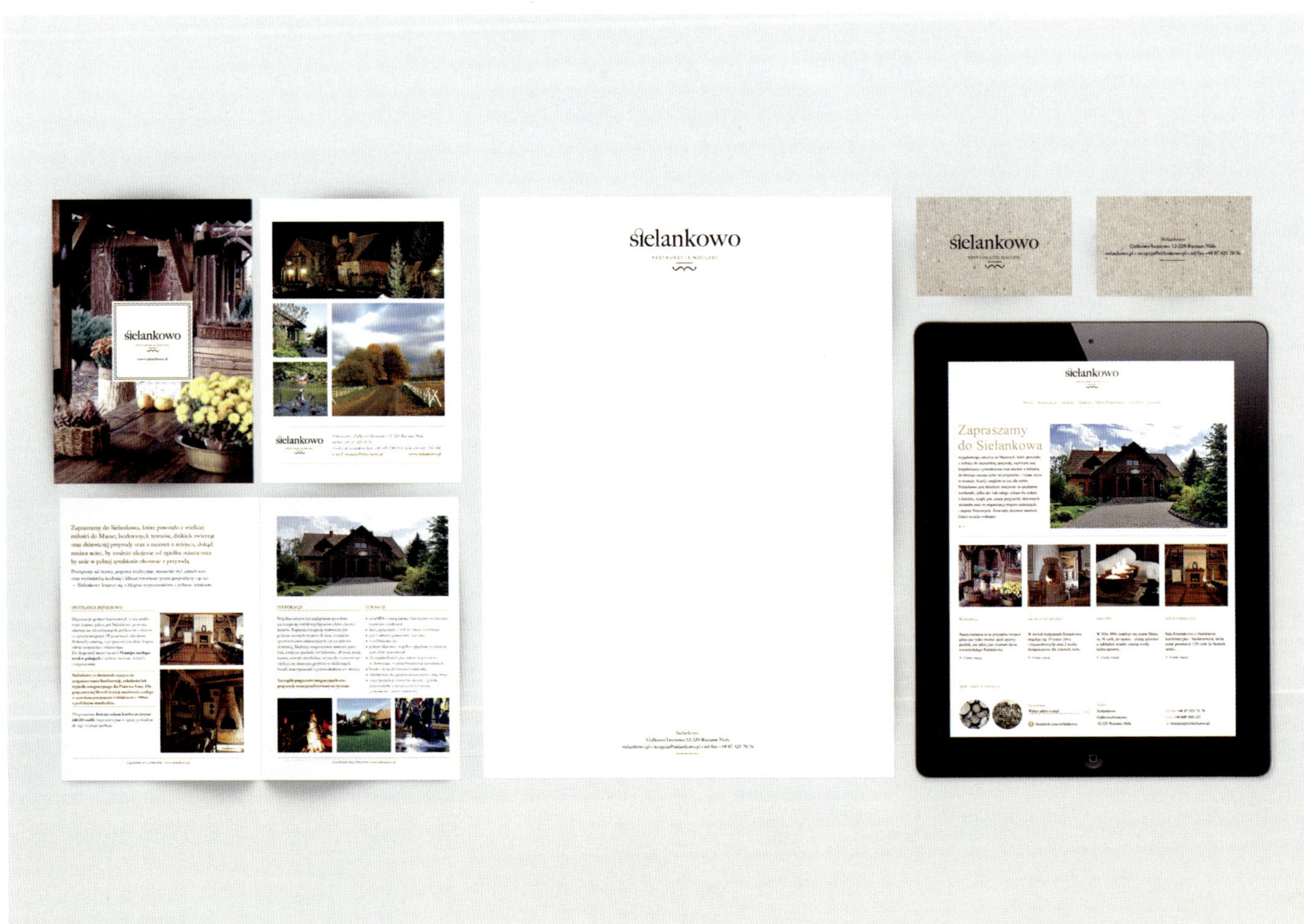

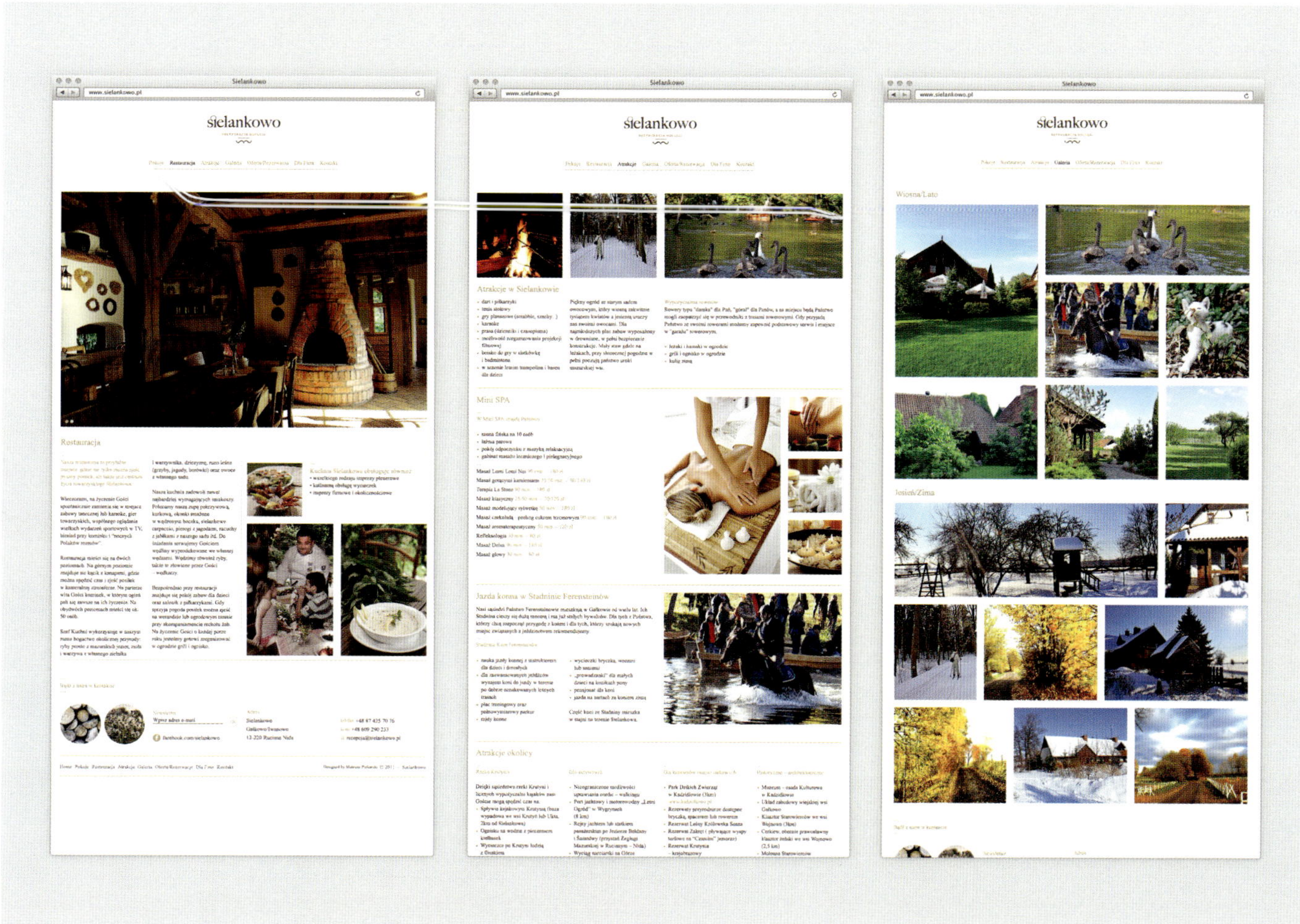

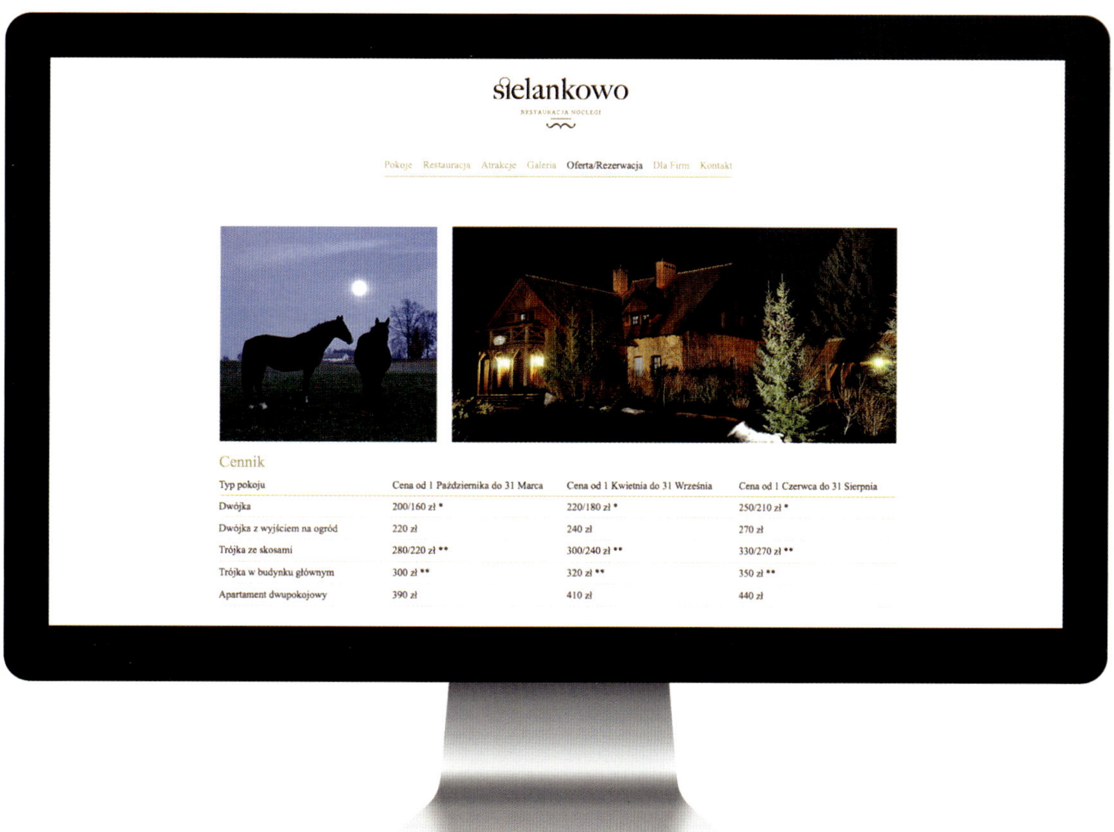
sielankowo
RESTAURACJA NOCLEGI
Pokoje Restauracja Atrakcje Galeria Oferta/Rezerwacja Dla Firm Kontakt
Cennik
Typ pokoju | Cena od 1 Października do 31 Marca | Cena od 1 Kwietnia do 31 Września | Cena od 1 Czerwca do 31 Sierpnia
Dwójka | 200/160 zł * | 220/180 zł * | 250/210 zł *
Dwójka z wyjściem na ogród | 220 zł | 240 zł | 270 zł
Trójka ze skosami | 280/220 zł ** | 300/240 zł ** | 330/270 zł **
Trójka w budynku głównym | 300 zł ** | 320 zł ** | 350 zł **
Apartament dwupokojowy | 390 zł | 410 zł | 440 zł

Only an hour and a half away from Beirut's City Center; Urban is situated in the Middle East's most exclusive region - Faqra.

Urban is a restaurant with eight individually designed rooms.

We were commissioned to design an identity for a surrealist interior.

All graphics were derived from Entopic graphomania - Entopic graphomania, is a surrealist and automatic method of drawing in which dots are made at the sites of impurities in a blank sheet of paper, and lines are then made between the dots.

This method was used for the logo, menus...

Solid bright colours were used to make the identity modern. Door signs were designed to be fun and interactive, witty signage was a big part of the identity, signs were placed in all rooms and no two were the same.

URBAN
FAQRA

Urban

Designer: Paperview Design / Lorette Shebaya
Client: Addmind
Location: Beirut

let there
be light

let there
be light

URBAN
PLEASE DON'T
TRASH THE ROOM.
THIS AIN'T VEGAS
URBAN
PLEASE DON'T
YELL IN THE HALL.
YOU MIGHT WAKE
THE DRAGON
URBAN
PLEASE DON'T
JUMP ON THE BED.
IT'S NOT YOUR
GRANDMA'S HOUSE
URBAN
PLEASE DON'T
START A FIRE.
OUR HEATING WORKS
URBAN
PLEASE DON'T
GO!!!!
WE LIKE HAVING YOU HERE
URBAN
PLEASE DON'T
RE-DECORATE.
WE HAVE SANDRA
FOR THAT
URBAN
PLEASE DON'T
HANG FROM
THE WINDOWS.
LEAVE THAT
TO SUPERMAN
URBAN
IF IT'S NOT YOURS
IT'S OURS

203

NOT YOUR ROOM

Chef Season, a culinary innovator, approached Accent when he opened his very first dessert-inspired cuisine restaurant - SEASON Cuisine Pâtissiartism. His picturesque dishes bring delicate blends of flavors to the palette and enchanting delights to the eyes.

Using Chef Season's favorite flower, the pansy, as the logo, Accent created a new identity and line of packaging for SEASON Cuisine Pâtissiartism. An illustrated pansy in conjunction to modern classic typography helps create a refined and elegant image that reflects the beauty and artistry of Chef Season's dishes.

SEASON Cuisine Pătissiartism

Design Agency: Accent Collective Inc.
Designer: Dennis Chang

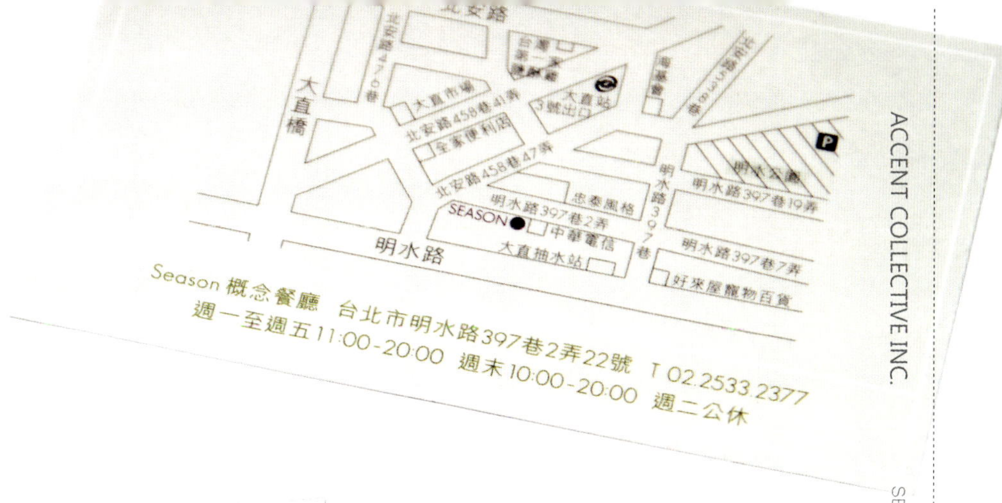
北安路
大直橋
明水路
SEASON
Season 概念餐廳 台北市明水路397巷2弄22號 T 02.2533.2377
週一至週五 11:00-20:00 週末 10:00-20:00 週二公休

SEASON
Cuisine Pâtissiartism

SEASON
Cuisine Pâtissiartism

Cuisine Pâtissiartism
SEASON

SEASON
Cuisine Pâtissiartism
概念餐廳

SEASON
Cuisine Pâtissiartism

SEASON
Cuisine Pâtissiartism

SEASON
SEASON
SEASON

VISUAL IMAGE DESIGN

HOTELS

The Shalom Hotel in Tel Aviv was totally rebuilt and renovated - and reborn as the Shalom & Relax, a beachhouse style boutique hotel. To deliver this idea, a set of patterns was created and used in a single-color palette throughout the hotel's visual communications. The result is a classy, sophisticated look & feel that is reflected by both the visual language and the hotel's interior design.

Shalom Hotel, Tel Aviv

Design Agency: Ada Rothenberg Design
Art director & Designer: Ada Rothenberg
Development: 'Vision Hospitality'
Client: Atlas Hotels, Israel
Photographer: Natan Dvir

welcome
SHALOM
hotel & relax

welcome
SHALOM
hotel & relax

Please
do not
disturb

שלום
SHALOM
hotel & relax

Markets
SHALOM
hotel & relax
Levards

SHALOM
hotel & relax
SHALOM
hotel & relax
SHALOM
hotel & relax
SHALOM
hotel & relax

The brand idea for this 50 room hotel is eclecticism: celebrating the thousand faces of Jerusalem, one of the oldest cities in the world. Photographer Natan Dvir and Ada Rothenberg went to the city to capture daily moments of its residents: Jewish orthodox and secular, Christian, Muslim, antique and modern.

The graphic identity is based on these photographs.

Harmony Hotel, Jerusalem

Design Agency: Ada Rothenberg Design
Art Director & Designer: Ada Rothenberg
Development: 'Vision Hospitality'
Client: Atlas Hotels, Israel
Photographer: Natan Dvir

3
סיור בירושלים: ארכיאולוגיה והיסטוריה
Tour in Jerusalem: Archaeology & History
2
סיור בירושלים: דתות
Day tour in Jerusalem: Religions
HARMONY
HOTEL
JERUSALEM

A new feel to an old city.
HARMONY
HOTEL
JERUSALEM

Dorchester Collection – Branding for a luxury hotel group

Design Agency: & SMITH

Dorchester Collection is a luxury hotel management company with a portfolio of nine iconic hotels around the world. By retaining the individuality of each hotel, the design palette allows the designers to combine Dorchester Collection's core brand colour - black - with colourful glimpses from each hotel's brand palette. High-production values and quality materials are employed across the brand, ensuring a tactile sense of luxury.

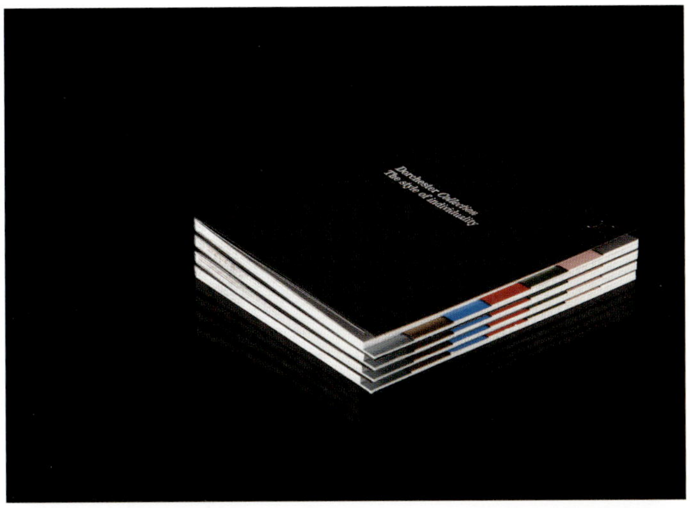
Dorchester Collection
The style of individuality

The Dorchester, London
The Beverly Hills Hotel, Beverly Hills
Le Meurice, Paris
Hôtel Plaza Athénée, Paris
Hotel Principe di Savoia, Milan
The New York Palace, New York
Hotel Bel-Air, Los Angeles
Coworth Park, Ascot (2010)
45 Park Lane, London (2010)

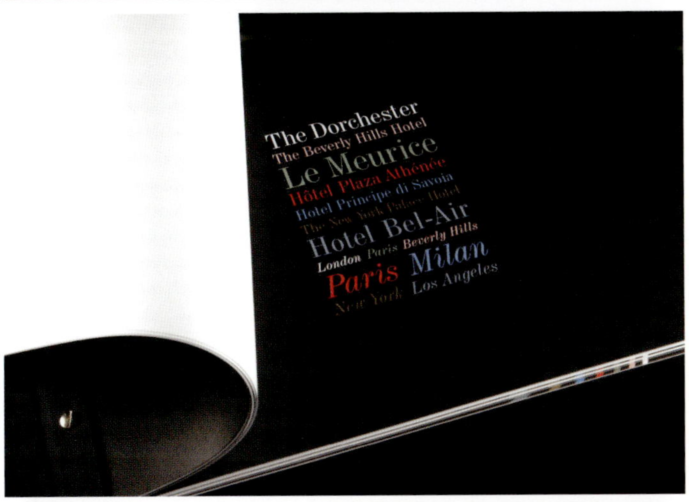
The Dorchester
The Beverly Hills Hotel
Le Meurice
Hôtel Plaza Athénée
Hotel Principe di Savoia
The New York Palace Hotel
Hotel Bel-Air
London Paris Beverly Hills
Paris Milan
New York Los Angeles

Dorchester Collection Vision
The ultimate hotel management company, with a passion for excellence and innovation, honouring the individuality and heritage of its iconic hotels

Coworth Park, Ascot
Opening mid 2010
At Coworth Park, we are reinventing the country house hotel for the 21st century. Set in 240 acres of picturesque parkland on the borders of historic Windsor Great Park, this rural idyll is only a short drive from central London and Heathrow Airport. With its groundbreaking eco-spa, Michelin-star chef, equestrian centre and polo fields, Coworth Park will blend the warmth and comfort of a traditional country house hotel with an eccentric spirit that is undeniably English and irrefutably modern.

Le Meurice
Rue de Rivoli, Paris

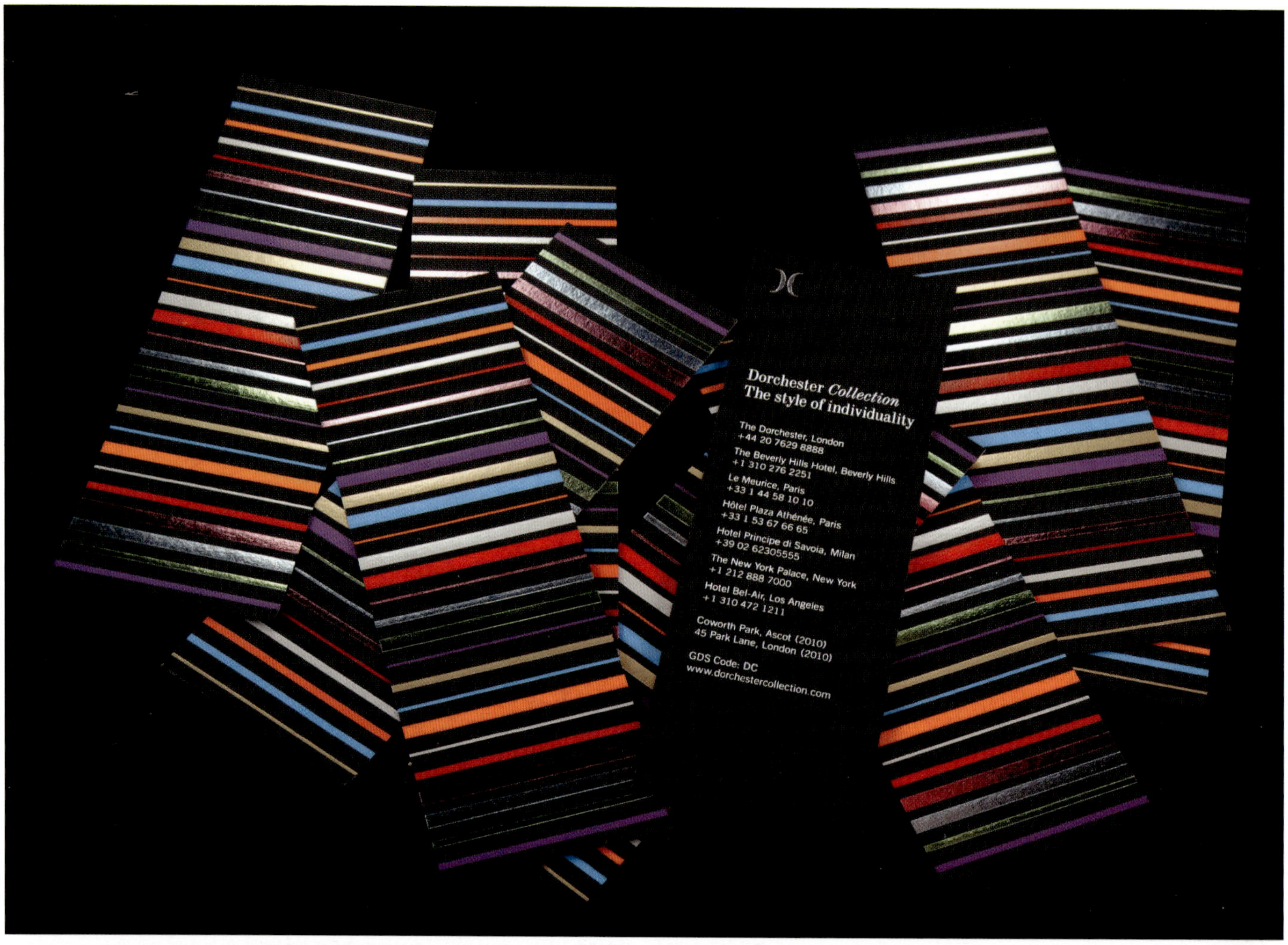
Dorchester *Collection*
The style of individuality
The Dorchester, London
+44 20 7629 8888
The Beverly Hills Hotel, Beverly Hills
+1 310 276 2251
Le Meurice, Paris
+33 1 44 58 10 10
Hôtel Plaza Athénée, Paris
+33 1 53 67 66 65
Hotel Principe di Savoia, Milan
+39 02 62305555
The New York Palace, New York
+1 212 888 7000
Hotel Bel-Air, Los Angeles
+1 310 472 1211
Coworth Park, Ascot (2010)
45 Park Lane, London (2010)
GDS Code: DC
www.dorchestercollection.com

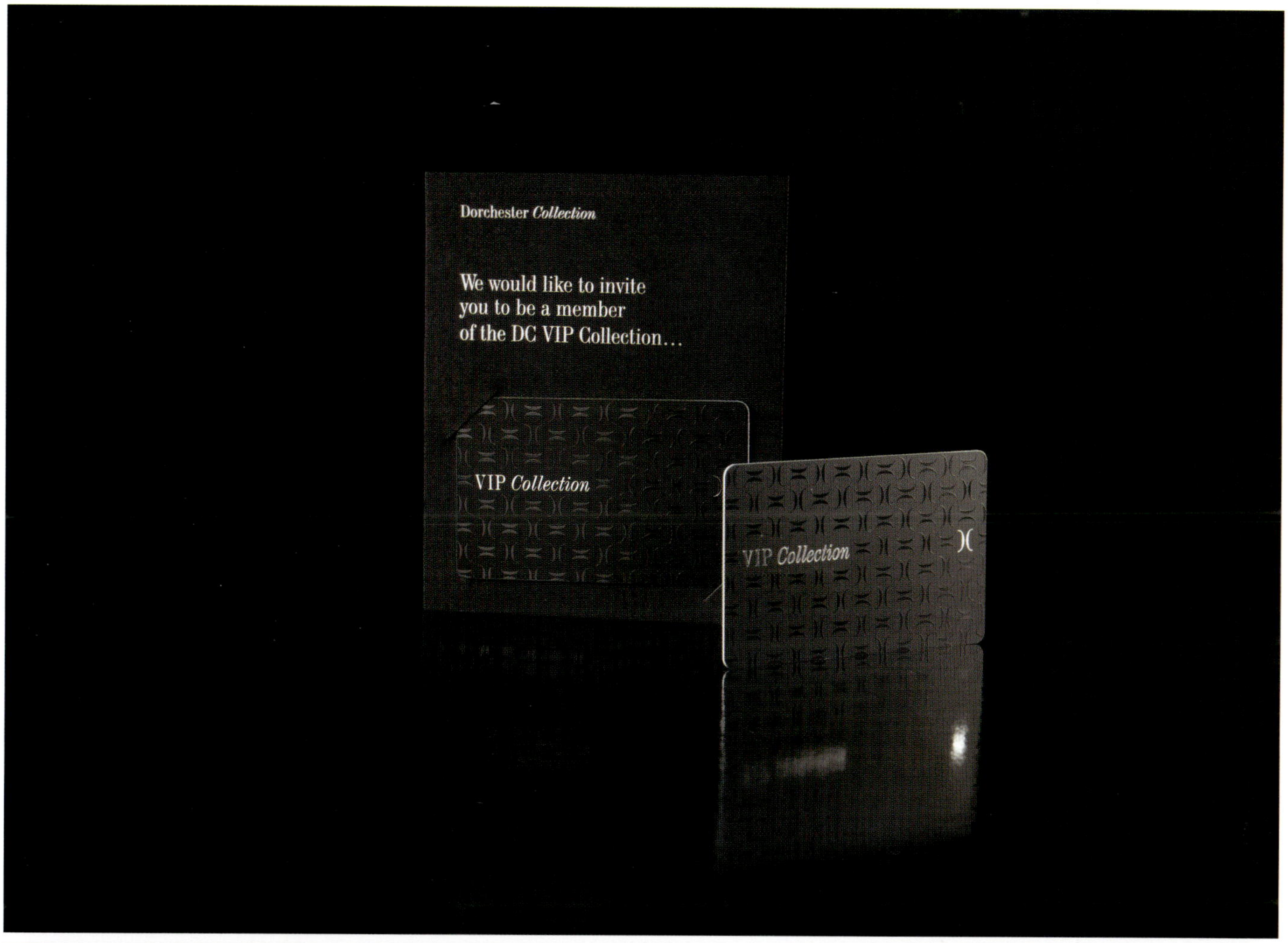
Dorchester Collection
We would like to invite you to be a member of the DC VIP Collection…
VIP Collection
VIP Collection

Martini Cool
The Beverly Hills Hotel Martini

The fine dining offer at Coworth Park, John Campbell at Coworth Park serves an innovative British menu courtesy of the acclaimed chef. Designed to distinguish the restaurant while complementing Coworth Park's look and feel, the identity suggests a refined tone appropriate to the restaurant's food and interiors. Led by an elegant logotype, ephemeral images of leaves (by photographer Giles Revell) and natural colours with copper accents, the identity hints at the surrounding countryside whilst suggesting the seasonal ingredients and intricate methods employed in John Campbell's cooking.

John Campbell at Coworth Park – Identity for a fine dining restaurant within a country hotel

Design Agency: & SMITH

JOHN CAMPBELL
AT COWORTH PARK

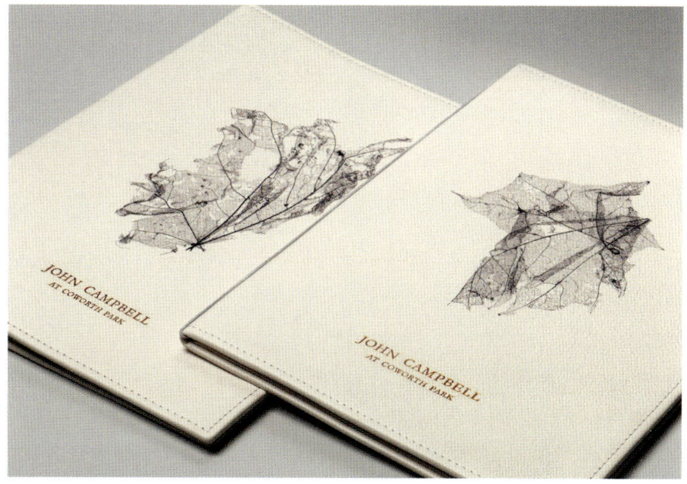

John Campbell at Coworth Park — Identity for a fine dining restaurant within a country hotel

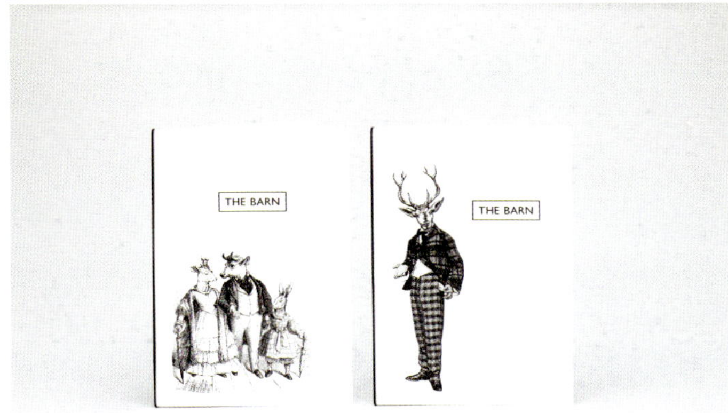

An informal restaurant at Coworth Park, The Barn offers exceptional seasonal fare courtesy of acclaimed chef John Campbell and his team. The identity & SMITH created for The Barn distinguishes it from the hotel's fine dining restaurant whilst retaining the Coworth Park look and feel. A bold logotype in a rectangular frame evokes a rustic, traditional tone reminiscent of agricultural 'brands'. This was combined with eccentric illustrations (animal heads attached to human bodies), sophisticated typography and warm, organic materials such as wood and brown leather.

The Barn – Identity for a restaurant within a country hotel

Design Agency: & SMITH

The Barn — Identity for a restaurant within a country hotel

In a play on words, Meridiano Sur refers to the long luminous geography of our country, Chile, that almost touches the world's South Pole. The development of the brand was focused on the enhancement of the architectural project of a typical chilean house and also in the innovative decoration that includes native handcrafts designs in order to provide a unique first experience into Chile.

Our amazing nature characterize us, from the desertic north to the antarctic ice, with its frame of high peaks from the Andes Mountains. Our fauna and flora is unique, diverse and also birthplace of outstanding poets, musicians and artists ranging from Nobel prize winners Pablo Neruda and Gabriela Mistral, to painter Roberto Matta and pianist Claudio Arrau.

The challenge was to develop an atmosphere inspired on the wooded surroundings of the Chilean diverse landscapes. The outcome is a petit hotel that brings to life embracing tree branches with winkles to our national nature; its varied scents and soothing scenarios.

With an incredible low budget we managed to bring our love to Chile on this pervasive graphic experience.

Through the visual identity we aimed to create a feeling of comfort and pleasure, providing tourists a travel experience and not just a lodging option. We wanted our guests to be living Chile from the first moment.

Meridiano Sur | Petit Hotel

Design Agency: Amenábar & Yávar

m
sur

meridiano
PETIT HOTEL
sur

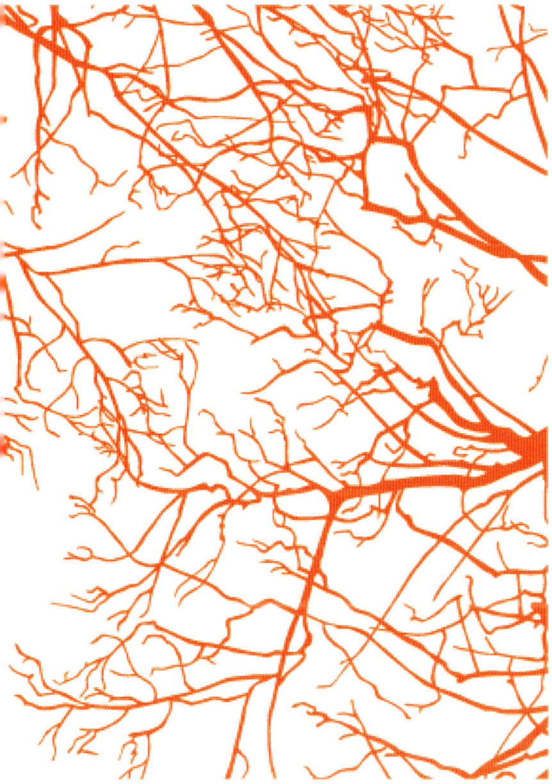

Juana Pérez Risopatrón
Gerente de Marketing
Santa Beatriz 256,
Providencia,
Santiago de Chile,
Sudamérica.
meridiano
petit hotel sur
Juana Pérez Risopatrón
Gerente de Marketing
Santa Beatriz 256,
Providencia,
Santiago de Chile,
Sudamérica.
meridiano
petit hotel sur

Hotel Lone is a showcase of Croatia's creative industry, with several of the nation's best architects, designers and artists involved in its creation. The hotel was designed by Zagreb's well known architecture studio 3LHD, and designers and artists involved in the project included Numen / For use, I-GLE, Silvio Vujičić and Ivana Franke.

The key visual is inspired by the central lobby, which is the most impressive volume of the hotel, extending along its entire height. This is a space that joins the hotel wings, contains all the most important facilities and is the origin of all activities. It is the "heart" of the hotel. That is why this space was selected as a symbol, whose form changes depending to which part of the hotel it is applied and the perspective from which it is viewed.

All the important applications are part of large 4-meter illustration created based on the visual identity. When combined, they create an integral image.

Hotel Lone

Design Agency: Bruketa&Žinić OM
Creative Director, Art Director: Davor Bruketa, Nikola Žinić
Art Director, Illustrator, Designer: Nebojša Cvetković
Designer: Sonja Šurbatović
Senior Copywriter: Ivan Čadež
Account Executive: Martina Ivkić
Production Manager: Vesna Durašin
DTP: Marko Ostrež, Radovan Radičević
Photographer: Domagoj Kunić, Marko Dabrović

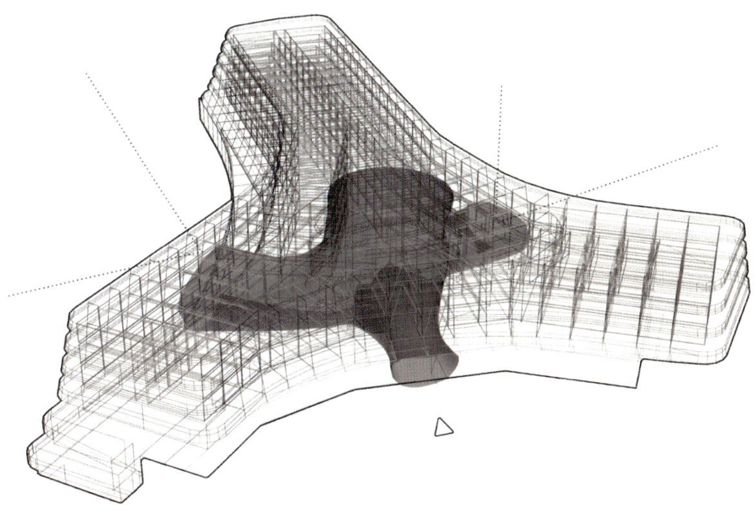

Visual identity of Hotel Lone

Hotel Lone is a display case for the creative industry of Croatia. It is a place for inspiration.

The key visual is inspired by the central lobby, which is the "heart" of the hotel.

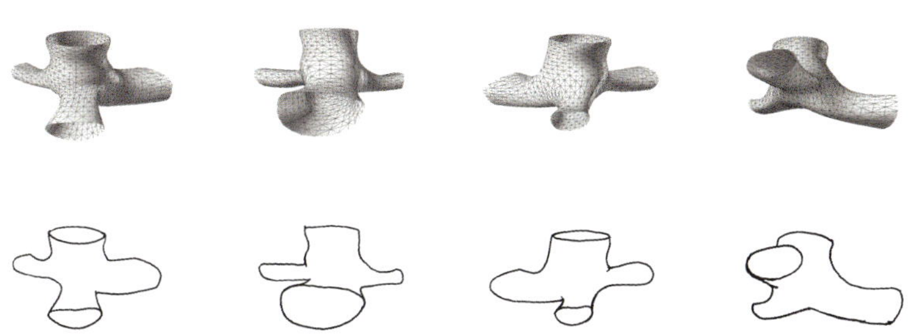

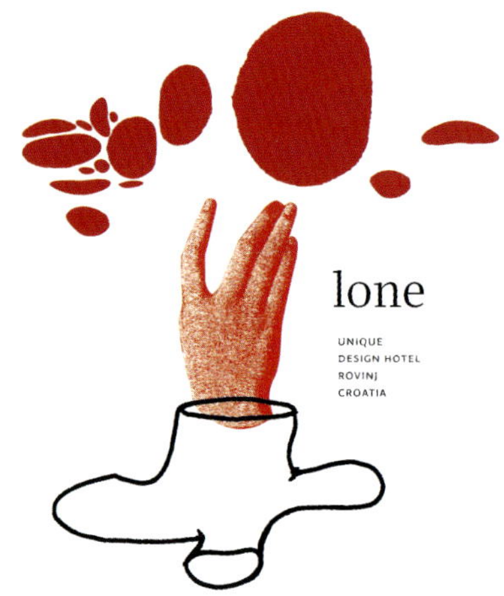
lone
UNIQUE
DESIGN HOTEL
ROVINJ
CROATIA

lone
UNIQUE
DESIGN HOTEL
ROVINJ
CROATIA

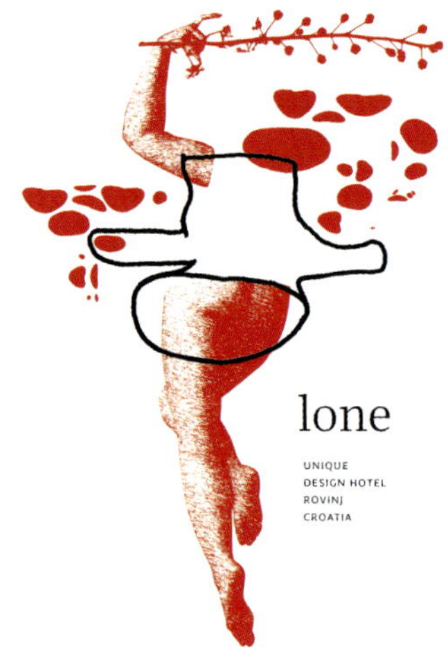
lone
UNIQUE
DESIGN HOTEL
ROVINJ
CROATIA

lone
UNIQUE
DESIGN HOTEL
ROVINJ
CROATIA

lone
UNIQUE
DESIGN HOTEL
ROVINJ
CROATIA

lone
UNIQUE
DESIGN HOTEL
ROVINJ
CROATIA

lone

lone
Wellness Bar

lone
Hotelske
informacije

lone
Kokteli
Cocktails

Night Club
lone
Night Club
Lone

Night Club
Night Club Lone

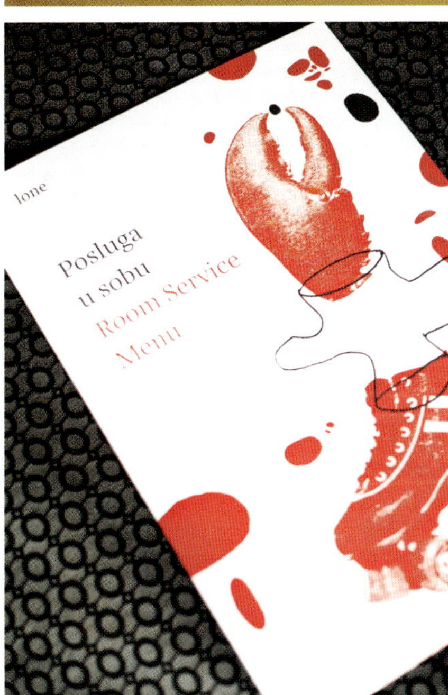
lone
Posluga
u sobu
Room Service
Menu

lone
Guest
Message
lone
Upitnik / Questionnaire

lone

lone

Molim vas,
pospremite sobu.
Hvala!
Please, make up
the room.
Thank you!
lone

Ne
ometaj!
Privacy
Please!
lone

Doručak
u sobi
Breakfast
menu

lone
lone

VIP Lounge
Restaurant
News

lone
Laku noć / Good Night

In an old sugar cane farmhouse called "Bethlehem", with extensive grounds full of greenery, pine and cane sugar fullfilled qwith colorful and natural wealth, existed the Big House (La Casona), the Little Castle and the beautiful gardens of the Salas family.

Some years after, during the 1950s, the family Telleria had the idea of turning La Casona into a guest house, named Belensate. This name is composed with the farmhouse name "Bethlehem" (Belen in spanish) and the family names Salas and Telleria.

Thus was born Hotel Belensate, and what was once a small inn surrounded by cane fields, is now a haven of memories and legends.

The visual identity program recreates and reflects the Hotel´s origins and feeling: gardens and natural materials, earth colors and textures, exotic beautiful flowers an vegetation, and colonial architecture.

The result is a smooth and delicate atmosphere that submerge the guests into the warm and yet elegant ambient of Belensate.

Hotel Belensate

Designer: Carmen Grisolía

Belensate
Urb. La Hacienda. Calle Principal No. 4-61
Telf. (master) +58 (274) 266.37.22
Fax Reserva: +58 (274) 266.75.55
Telefax: +58 (274) 266.12.55
Mérida. Edo. Mérida - Venezuela
www.hotelbelensate.com
hotelbelensate@cantv.net
RIF: J-09004587-2

Paz y Tranquilidad
Peace & Quiet
Pace e Tranquilità
Paix et Tranquilitè
Frieden und Ruhe
Limpio y Fresco
Clean & Fresh
Pulito e Fresco
Je nettoie et Frais
Sauber und Frisch

Nuestro Hotel cuenta con un total de 99 habitaciones, distribuidas entre habitaciones sencillas, matrimoniales, suites y cabañas, completamente equipadas con servicio de televisión por cable e internet.
En el Bar La Fontana, Usted podrá disfrutar del paisaje natural mientras degusta de sus comidas al aire libre.
Le ofrecemos también nuestros servicios de tienda, souvenirs y Agencia de Viajes.
Para cualquier información o reservaciones comuníquese con nosotros a nuestros teléfonos en horario de oficina, o por nuestra dirección web.
La Era Restaurant ofrece lo mejor de la gastronomía internacional para el deleite de los paladares más exigentes. En nuestro bar podrá degustar de las mejores bebidas y los cocteles más exquisitos, acompañado de un excelente ambiente musical.
Nuestros salones para banquetes y conferencias le darán la oportunidad de transformar los eventos que Ud. planifique en momentos especiales e inolvidables.
Nuestros servicios le garantizan una estadía placentera.

En una vieja hacienda de caña de azúcar llamada "Belén", con extensos terrenos llenos de vegetación, pinos y caña de azúcar de gran colorido y riquezas naturales, existía la Gran Casona, el Pequeño Castillo y los bellísimos jardines de los señores Salas.
Un buen día los señores Tellería tuvieron la idea de construir en la Casona una posada. Ésta se inició en el año 1950 con el nombre de Belensate. Este nombre se compone con el de la Hacienda Belén y los apellidos Salas y Tellería.
Así nace el Hotel Belensate, y lo que antes fue la pequeña posada rodeada de cañaverales, es hoy un paraíso de recuerdos y leyendas.
Urb. La Hacienda. Calle Principal No. 4-61.
Telf. (master) +58 (274) 266.37.22
Fax Reserva: +58 (274) 266.75.55
Telefax: +58 (274) 266.12.55.
Mérida. Edo. Mérida - Venezuela.
Website: www.hotelbelensate.com
hotelbelensate@cantv.net . RIF: J-09004587-2
Belensate
El Hotel de Mérida

Hotel Belensate

Belensate
Urb. La Hacienda. Calle Principal No. 4-61. Telf. (master) +58 (274) 266.37.22 - Fax Reserva: +58 (274) 266.75.55 - Telefax: +58 (274) 266.12.55.
Mérida. Edo. Mérida - Venezuela. Website: www.hotelbelensate.com - hotelbelensate@cantv.net . RIF: J-09004587-2

Belensate
Por favor botar el papel
sólo en la papelera

Belensate
Sauna

• esterilizado • sterilizzato • sterilized • sterilisert • esterilizado • sterilizzato • sterilized • sterilisert •

The "Posada Doña Pumpa" is a small and cozy Bed & Breakfast located in Mérida, Venezuela.

The family house was redecorated to make it a wonderful guesthouse, carrying the name of the beloved Pumpa, the grandmother the house is filled with memories and a homey atmosphere, as well as remembrances and antique decoration.

The concept for this work is based in the expression "Feel at home", and the logo features a capital "P" that resembles an antique key, with the touch of confidence that comes from giving guests the key to our own home and makes them feel like they are in home as well.

The overall look and feel is designed to recreate an antique colonial house in Venezuelan 1900´s century tradition, using the mosaic tiles and vintage photography as resources for the construction of this homey environment.

Posada Doña Pumpa

Dedien Agency: Medina & Grisolía
Designer: Carmen Grisolía and Jhonatan Medina Caguana

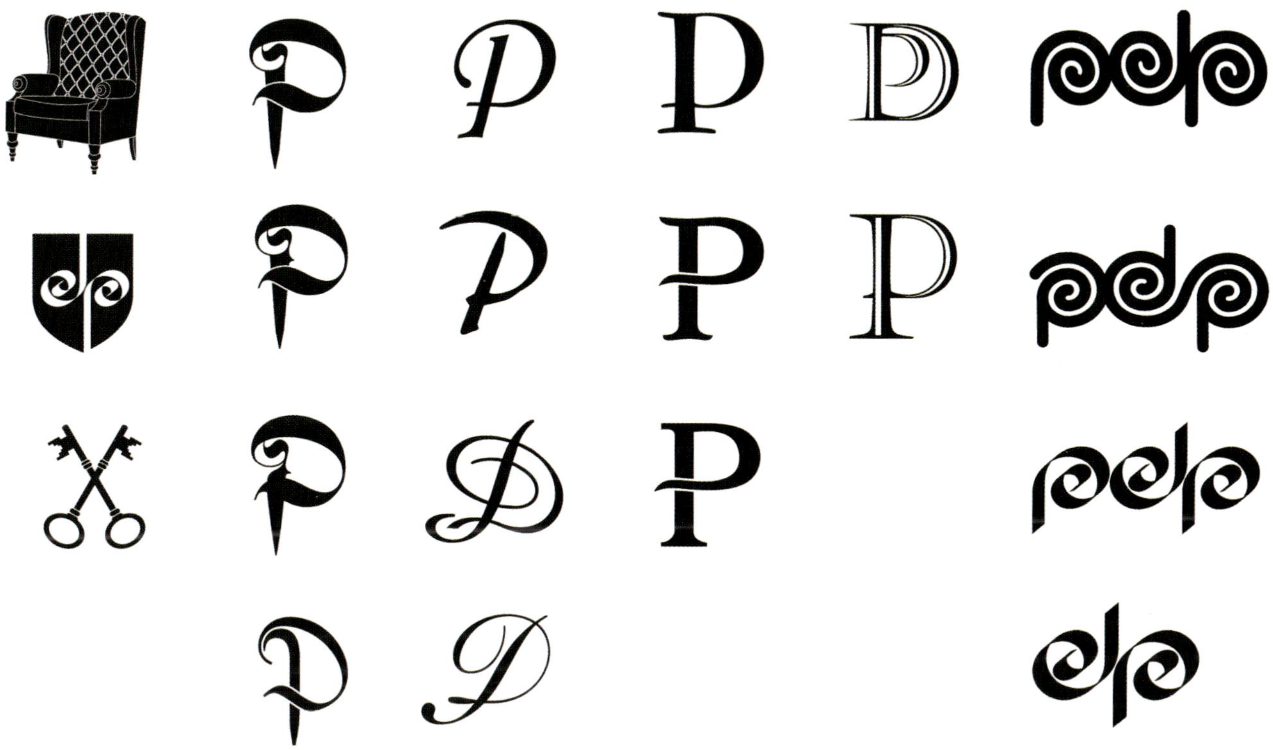

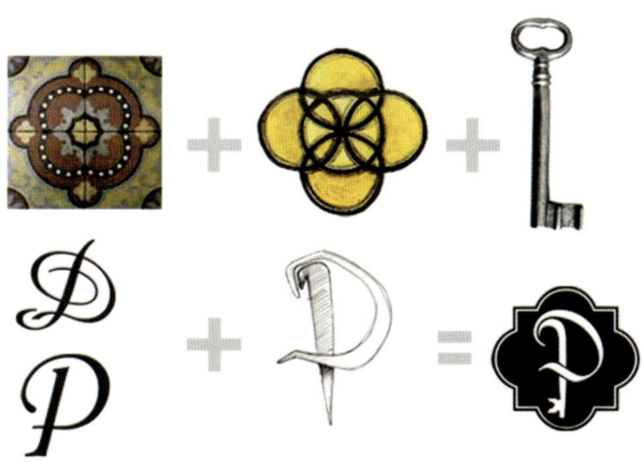

ABCDE

LOREM IPSUM DOLOR SIT AMET, CONSECTETUR ADIPISCING ELIT. INTEGER SIT AMET TINCIDUNT LOREM. INTEGER A ENIM A NEQUE ULLAMCORPER ELEIFEND. QUISQUE TEMPOR

LOREM IPSUM DOLOR SIT AMET, CONSECTETUR ADIPISCING ELIT. INTEGER SIT AMET TINCIDUNT LOREM. INTEGER A ENIM A NEQUE ULLAMCORPER ELEIFEND. QUISQUE TEMPOR .

Pellentesque justo neque, auctor quis hendrerit vitae, tempus eget magna. Sed id lobortis augue. Nam pharetra sagittis leo, id vehicula elit

1
2
3
4
5

Helvetica

ABCDEFGHJKLM
NÑOPQRSTUVW
XYZ
abcdefghijklmnño
pqrstuvwxyz

CHARLEMAGNE

ABCDEFGHIJ
KLMNÑOPQR
STUVWXYZ

CHARLEMAGNE SDT BOLD

ABCDEFGHIJ
KLMNÑOPQR
STUVWXYZ

C: 100 M: 86 Y:13 K:2
R:0 G: 73 B: 144
Web: 002671
L: 30 a: 01 b: 49

C: 0 M: 27 Y:76 K:0
R:252 G: 189 B: 148
Web: ffbc3a
L: 30 a: 01 b: 49

C: 0 M: 27 Y:76 K:0
R:58 G: 76 B: 0
Web: ffbc3a
L: 74 a: 100 b: 29

DOÑA PUMPA
POSADA

DOÑA PUMPA
POSADA

DOÑA PUMPA
POSADA

Habitación

Habitación

Habitación
→

Conserje

Cocina

Cocina
→

Teléfono

Lobby

Recepción
→

Recepción

Estacionamiento

Estacionamiento
→

Baños

Baños

Baños
→

Gimnasio

Servicios

Sala de Juegos

7

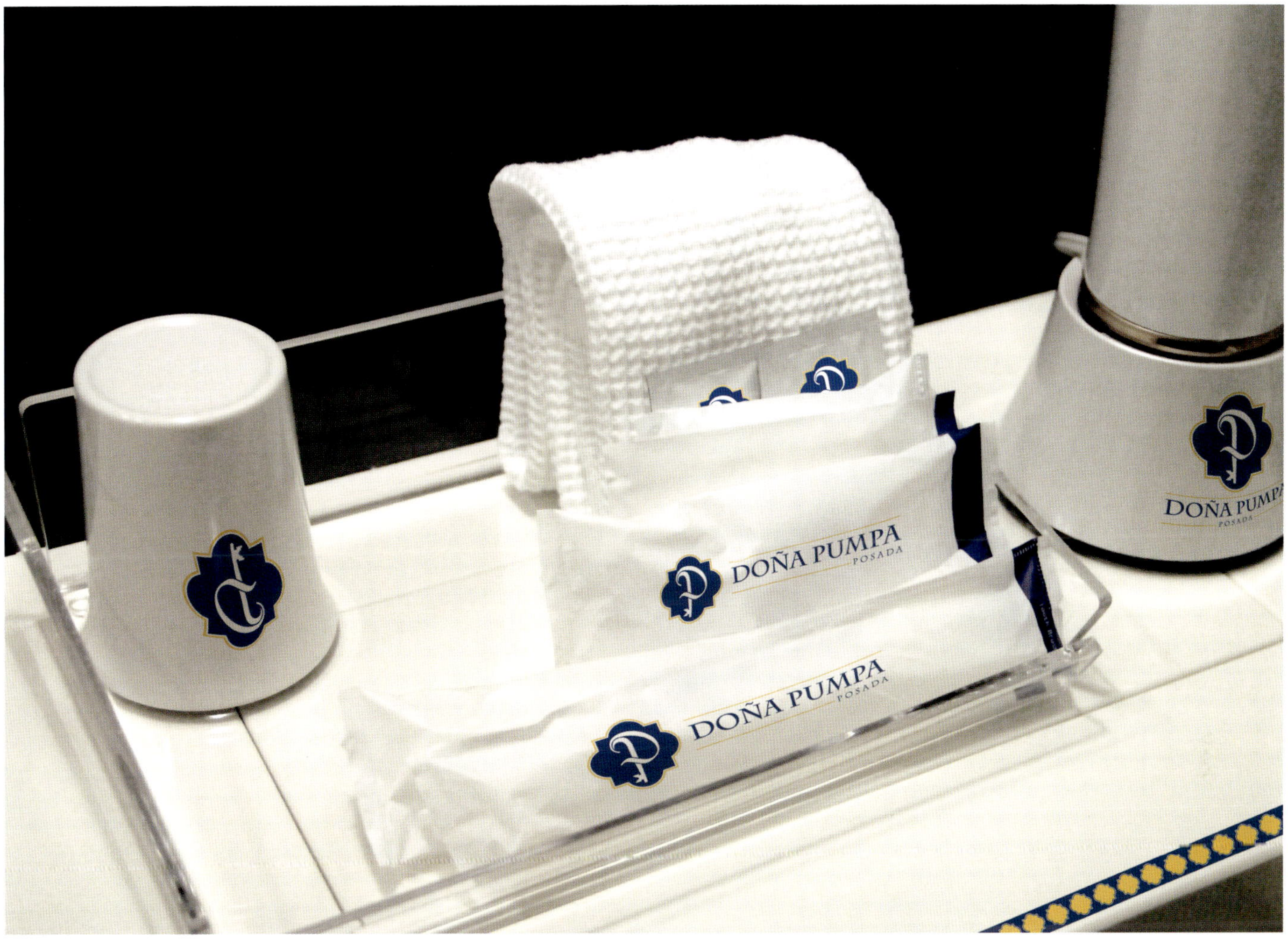
DOÑA PUMPA
POSADA
DOÑA PUMPA
POSADA

DOÑA PUMPA
Sr. Leonardo Montilla
Augusto Fuentes Medina
DOÑA PUMPA
POSADA

DOÑA PUMPA
POSADA
DOÑA PUMPA
DOÑA PUMPA
Identidad Visual
Identidad Visual

Located in the Old Main District of Starkville, MS, Hotel Chester is a registered historic site in a small Southern town. The identity reflects the period when the hotel was established, during the Prohibition era of the 1920's. The packaging design for the in-room hygiene products is reminiscent of a cigar box, the interior of which is wrapped with vintage halftone images of Main Street, circa 1924, printed on linen.

Hotel Chester

Designer: Cristina Jucan

HOTEL
CHESTER
HC

HOTEL
CHESTER
SHAMPOO
CONDITIONER
HOTEL
CHESTER
BODY
OIL
HOTEL
CHESTER
BODY
WASH
HC

HOTEL
CHESTER

The Dee Why Hotel is back after a three-year refurbishment break. A sumptuous new space designed by SJB, Deuce redesigned the identity with a custom type treatment. Hand-created elements appear over signage, print and uniforms in an extensive rollout.

Dee Why Hotel

Design Agency: Deuce Design

MENU
DeeWhy
-Hotel-
LUNCH
SHARE
DINNER
DESSERTS
SIDES

MENU
DeeWhy
-Hotel-

DeeWhy
-Hotel-

DeeWhy
-Hotel-

TAP
MENU
DeeWhy
MENU

MENU
DeeWhy
-Hotel-

Located on the southern shore of Sydney Harbour, immediately north-west of the Sydney central business district, The Rocks precinct was the historic centre of Australia's first European settlement in 1788. The Harbour Rocks Hotel (HRH) is situated within this busy tourist and city worker hub and surrounded by cobbled paving and sandstone stores.

The Harbour Rocks Hotel custom identity directly references and draws inspiration from the hotels' historical past as a first settler store converted into a boutique hotel. The black and white historical images, used extensively in the stationery collateral, were taken in 1901 in Harrington Street, Sydney. The imageused in the business cards is a historical map of the area drawn in 1802. The identity is a combination of warm brown and gold tones reminiscent of the surrounding historical architecture, the Sydney Harbour Bridge and the Sandstone blocks. The custom typeface is contemporary yet draws on a retro-combo-vintage aesthetic. The entire identity package complements the hotel's new makeover and breathes life into one of Sydney's oldest boutique hotels.

The extensive collateral included all external and internal hotel signage, bar and restaurant branding, signage and menu systems and extensive room and hotel stationery packs.

Harbour Rocks Hotel Identity

Design Agency: Deuce Design

←Harbour View Suite
Rooms 310-316

Scarlett Restaurant
Terrace
Gym
Rooms 101-104 ↘

SCARLETT

Brand identity work for Hotel Milano Scala, a 4-star Superior property located in the heart of Milan, and this work including logo, corporate identity, stationery, leaflet, brochure, website design and development.

Hotel Milano Scala

Design Agency: Elever
Designer: Luca Cairoli, Egidia Cassinese, Martina Facco

Pochi minuti a piedi da:
Walking distance from:
TEATRO ALLA SCALA 3 min
CASTELLO SFORZESCO
PINACOTECA DI BRERA
BRERA NIGHTLIFE
FASHION DISTRICT
TEATRO ALLA SCALA
GALLERIA VITTORIO EMANUELE II
DUOMO
FINANCIAL DISTRICT
Hotel Milano Scala
via dell'Orso, 7
20121 Milano
www.hotelmilanoscala.it
info@hotelmilanoscala.it
Ufficio di preapertura
Pre-opening office

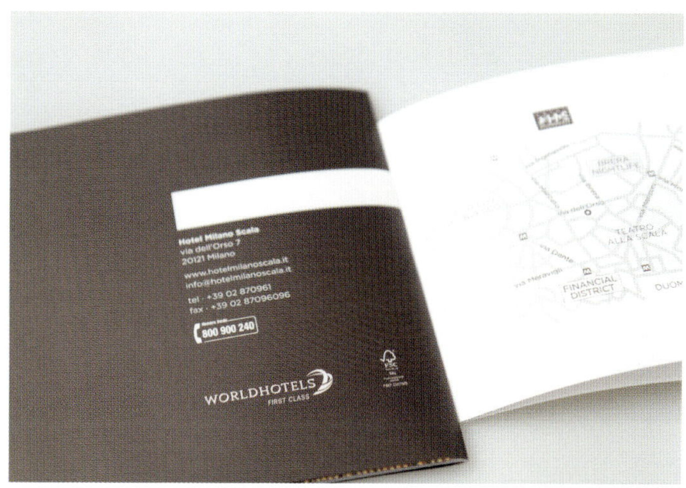
Hotel Milano Scala
via dell'Orso 7
20121 Milano
www.hotelmilanoscala.it
info@hotelmilanoscala.it
tel · +39 02 870961
fax · +39 02 87096096
800 900 240
WORLDHOTELS
FIRST CLASS

Appunti di viaggio · Travel notes

The look and feel of the project was inspired by Elissa's mother, Hazel. Elissa used her pictures of her mother and other family photos on recycled paper and organic fabrics to create a vintage feel. Hazelwood Hotel is an eco-friendly boutique hotel that represents luxury without excess. The focus is giving the guest everything they need with a consciousness of the world around them.

Hazelwood Hotel Branding

Designer: Elissa Shapiro

Hazelwood

DO NOT DISTURB

PLEASE MAKE UP THE ROOM

ROOM SERVICE MENU
Hazelwood
ENJOY A LITTLE R&R
BRING THE FAM
SPEND TIME WITH YOUR SWEETHEART
Hazelwood
BRING THE KIDS
Hazelwood
LET THE GOOD TIMES ROLL
Hazelwood

The old Red Eagle Hotel was a cultural cringe in Albert Park. We were approached with the question; '... keep the name or re-brand?' Rather than try to re-badge the existing venue, Hotel Nest was hatched. The owner's brief was to create a European inspired, modern yet whimsical look and feel.

Ennis & Perry developed a new identity and brand that reflected the surrounding environment, as well as addressing the owner's vision for the new establishment. Working closely with the architects, we also designed environmental graphics for the exterior and interiors.

Our work for Hotel Nest has included brand and identity design, Interior graphics, illustrations, wayfinding, content managed websites, newsletter marketing and customer subscription database, along with press advertising and promotional marketing.

Hotel Nest

Design Agency: Ennis Perry Creative

hotelnest
ABN 89 122 965 002 ACN 122 965 002
111 Victoria Ave, Albert Park 3206
T 03 9699 9744
F 03 9699 9981
E enquiries@hotelnest.com.au
www.hotelnest.com

Menu
Wines

hotelnest

hôtel nest
Spring Carnival
Derby Day Races
Derby Day at Hotel Nest
Melbourne Cup Day
Oaks Day
Ticket Price $30 (limited tickets)
Door Entry $10
2 Course Set Menu $50pp
Ticket Price $30

Saturday
27th September
from midday
GRAND
FINAL
DAY
FREE
BEER
until first goal
SEE ALL THE ACTION ON
3 LARGE TV
SCREENS
> FREE BEER until first goal
> FREE BEER until the first goal
in 2nd half of the game
> FOUR'N TWENTY PIES available all day
> LIVE BAND after the game
> GRAND FINAL RECOVERY on Sunday
- Resident gig - Russell Robertson from 7pm
hôtelnest
111 Victoria Avenue Albert Park 3206
T +613 9699 9744 | E enquiries@hotelnest.com.au | www.hotelnest.com.au

Cantera Diez is a Hotel Boutique located in the heart of Morelia, Mexico.

The Hotel features eleven suites of exquisite design, elegance and comfort hosted in a newly renovated 18th century building.

It provides an atmosphere of perfect balance between the modern style of its interiors and the colonial flavor of its architecture.

Cantera Diez

Designer: Erika Magallon

CANTERA DIEZ
HOTEL-BOUTIQUE

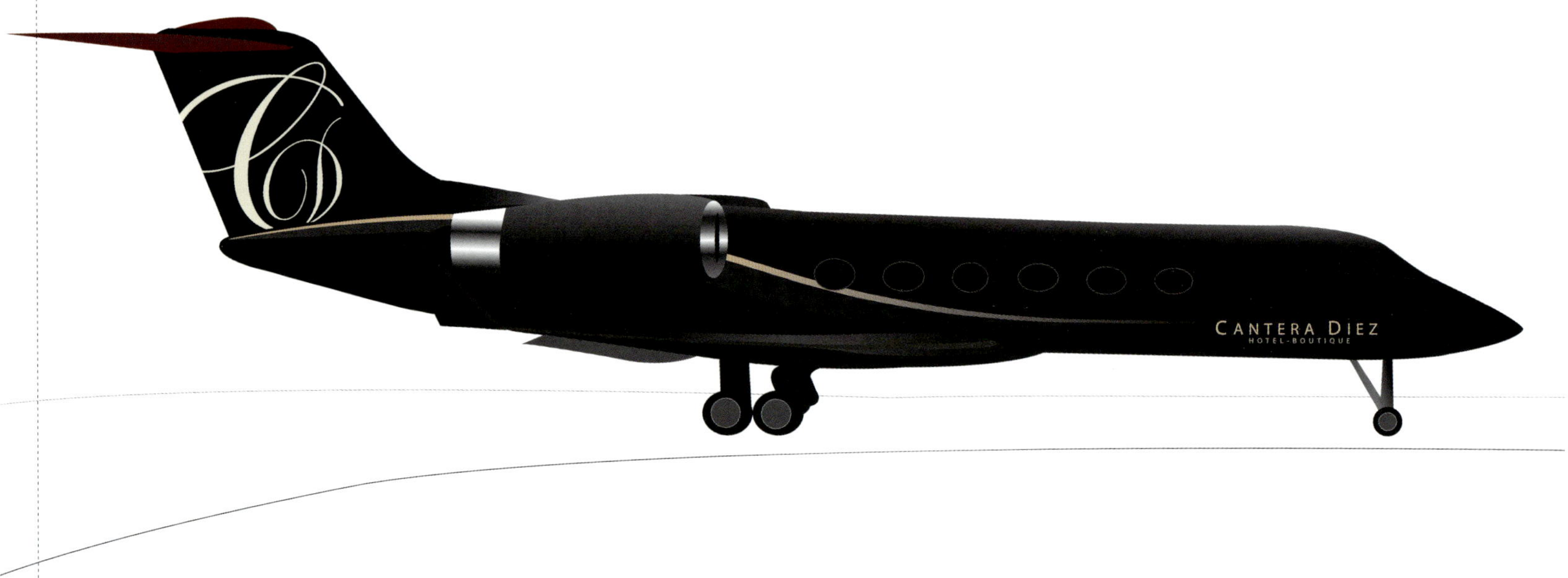

SHAMPOO
CANTERA DIEZ
CONDITIONER
CANTERA DIEZ

Wanderlust as the dictionary defines is a strong innate desire to travel.

The custom made logotype expresses the feeling of dreaminess, fantasy and the discovery of the surreal landscape of a new world. The dash lines evoke the impulse to join the lines, as with the impulse to travel. The act of joining the lines is also analogous with the marking of lines from point to point, as with what a traveler would want to do on his map to plan or track his route.

The airmail tricolor band is synonymous with traveling and correspondence- the conveyance of the emotions and thoughts kindled during a journey via mail.

The brand attributes conveyed by the brand mark are: whimsical, elegant, happy, unexpected yet familiar and comforting. Various forms of ephemerals and keepsakes experienced during a journey were carefully studied, thought-out and deployed onto the collateral set. Bus ticket for rate cards; air ticket for brochure inserted into an "air-ticket wallet"; notebook aptly named "ITINERARY" as a multi-purposeful room-directory/ guide book/journal for the guests...etc.

Wanderlust, Singapore

Design Agency: Foreign Policy Design Group
Creative Director & Art Director: Yah-Leng Yu
Designer: Yah-Leng Yu, Tianyu Isaiah Zheng (TY) & May Lim
Illustrator: Cheryl Chong
Client: Wanderlust, Singapore
Photographer: Michael Tan (Mika Images)

Wanderlust, Singapore

Wanderlust, Singapore

Wanderlust, Singapore

The Opera Garden Hotel & Apartments is perfect for those, who would like to have some rest as well as visiting the exciting centre of Budapest. The reconstructed hotel waits its guests with contemporary designed apartments. The identity of hotel perfectly reflects the atmosphere of the past century and still harmonizes with the "green" modernism of the building.

Opera Garden Hotel & Apartments Identity

Design Agency: Graphasel Design Studio
Designer: László Ördögh, Dóra Vágfalvi, Péter Szöke, David Drozsnyik, Attila Bolgár, Zsuzsa Nonn
Client: Opera Garden Hotel & Apartments
Location: Hungary
Photographer: Attila Balázs

OPERA-GARDEN
HOTEL & APARTMENTS

FEEL AT HOME IN THE CITY
OPERA-GARDEN

OPERA-GARDEN
HOTEL & APARTMENTS
OPERA GARDEN HOTEL
& APARTMENTS

AZ OPERA GARDEN HOTEL & APARTMENTS BUDAPEST SZÍVÉBEN, EGY SÉTÁLÓUTCÁBAN TALÁLHATÓ, NÉHÁNY HÁZTÖMBRE AZ OPERAHÁZTÓL
Exkluzív szolgáltatásaival az OPERA GARDEN HOTEL & APARTMENTS egyedülálló kombinációja egy négy csillagos butik hotelnek és egy barátságos, nyugodt légkörű apartman szállodának.
A 35 egyedileg kialakított szoba és apartman biztosítja a legmagasabb szintű kényelmet, amely lehetővé teszi, hogy Ön vendégközpontú és professzionális kiszolgálás mellett élvezze a szálloda összes szolgáltatását.

OPERA-GARDEN
HOTEL & APARTMENTS

Royal Park Boutique Hotel Identity

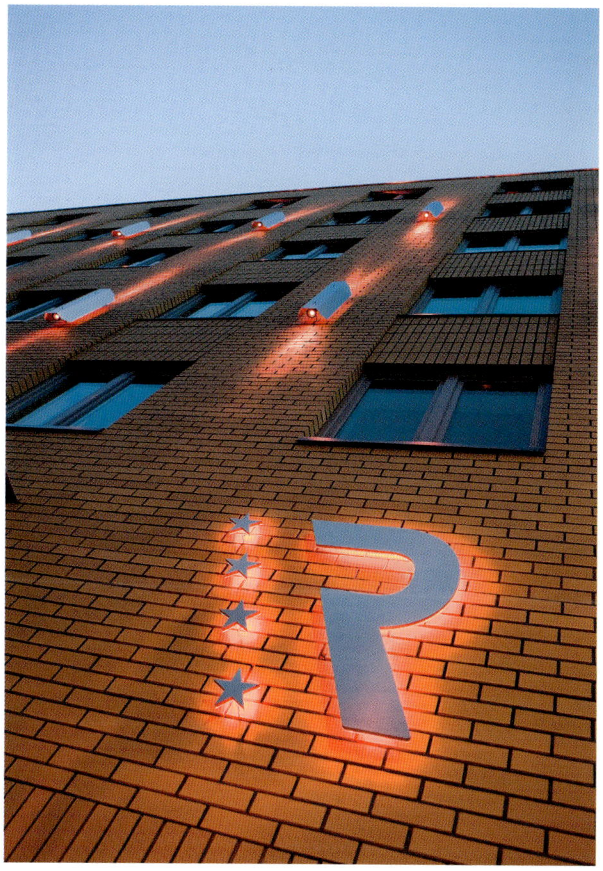

Since the Hotel primarily aimed to invite young tourists, we decided to design a spectacular and striking identity. We used pictograms to indicate the function of all pieces of equipment which, besides providing a funny appearance, also emphasizes functionality. The front light was accomplished by using environment-friendly LED technology, the concept of which fits well into the identity that primarily uses recycled materials.

Royal Park Boutique Hotel Identity

Design Agency: Graphasel Design Studio
Designer: László Ördögh, Dóra Vágfalvi, Péter Szöke, David Drozsnyik, Zsuzsa Nonn, Attila Bolgár, Sándor Polyák
Client: Royal Park Boutique Hotel
Photographer: Attila Balázs

BOUTIQUE HOTEL
PÉTER HERCSE
Front Office Manager
Nefelejcs u. 6. H-1078
Tel.: +36 1 872 8888 ★ Fa
www.royalparkboutiquehote
frontofficemanager@royalpar
VÁROSLIGET
Dózsa György út
Felvonulási tér
Damjanich utca
Peterdy utca
Városliget fasor
Hernád utca
Ajtósi Dürer sor
István utca
Abonyi utca

ROYAL PARK BOUTIQUE HOTEL
Nefelejcs u. 6. H-1078 Budapest, Hungary
Tel.: +36 1 872 8888 ★ Fax: +36 1 872 8889
www.royalparkboutiquehotel.hu
reservation@royalparkhotel.hu
Name
Room Number
Signature
Arrival Date

Welcome to the Royal Park Boutique Hotel
CHECK OUT TIME IS 11 AM
ROYAL PARK
BOUTIQUE
HOTEL
Name
Room Number
Arrival Date
Departure Date

700 HUF

We undertook to design a comprehensive visual communication for the Hotel. Besides the materials presented here, the decoration of rooms, as well as the design of the hotel uniform was also included in our work. The main expectation of our Client was to create a fresh and lovely environment that reflects on the lively life in Budapest.

Soho Hotel Identity

Design Agency: Graphasel Design Studio
Designer: László Ördögh, David Drozsnyik, Dóra Vágfalvi, Péter Szöke, Zsuzsa Nonn, Attila Bolgár
Client: Soho Hotel
Location: Hungary
Photograper: Attila Balázs

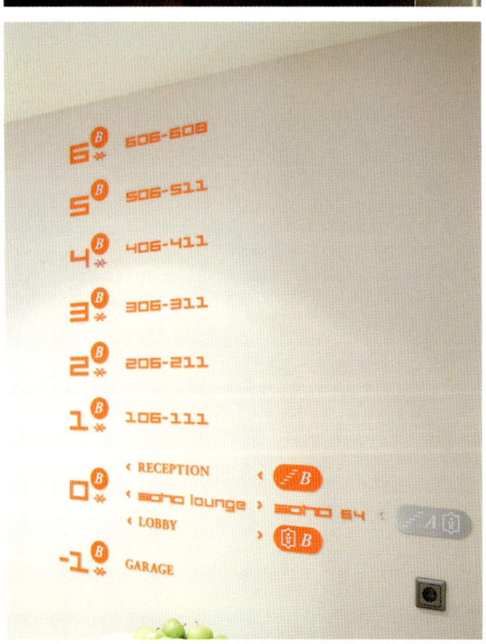

"of Budapest"
soho
HOTEL
www.sohohotel.hu
Member of

San Francisco-based Personality Hotels is home to some of the city's first boutique hotels. Having grown over many decades, the company's old identity and collateral lacked cohesiveness and didn't properly represent their hotel family. After an extensive in-person visit to each hotel, brand analysis, and customer and staff interviews, Noise 13 discovered that personal experience was the key to the company and the brand creating a strategy towards a more cohesive brand package.

Since Personality Hotels was undergoing major overhauls in three of their hotels, it was the perfect time to give their parent brand a face-lift while we worked on the individual hotels' branding. A redesigned corporate logo, new messaging, print collateral, and graphic standards better aligned them with their target markets and unified the family of hotels. We also developed identity and in-room materials for the individual hotels (Hotel Frank, Hotel Vertigo, Hotel Union Square) as well as a refresh of materials for Hotel Diva and the Kingston Park Hotel.

HOTEL FRANK

personality hotels
SAN FRANCISCO

Pesonality Hotels

Design Agency: Noise 13

IN
THE BED
OUT
ON THE TOWN
HOTEL UNION SQUARE

my freshly reimagined, modern makeover by designer riley johndonnell. i've kept my historic qualities, but enhanced my loft-like rooms with striking graphic styling and state-of-the-art technology, inspiring you to experience san francisco in comfort and luxury.
I AM HOTEL UNION SQUARE.
MODERN.
SPACIOUS.
personality hotels

HOTEL FRANK
386 Geary Street
San Francisco, CA 94102
415.986.2000 tel
415.397.2447 fax
www.personalityhotels.com
1.800.553.1900 reservations
personality hotels
COLLECTION

HOTEL FRANK.
ABSOLUTE FABULIST
152 GUEST ROOMS
2 ROOFTOP PENTHOUSE SUITES
Custom Furniture
Meeting Space
Entirely Non-Smoking
Pet-Friendly
Valet Parking
Daily Newspaper
Complimentary Wi-Fi
Business Center
"Max's On The Square" Restaurant On Premises
Eco-Practices
Honor Bar
Flat-Screen TVs with HD Programming
Extended Pillow Selection
Signature Robes & Slippers
iPod Speaker Docks
Dual Cordless Phones
In-Room Climate Control
Evening Turn-Down
Access to Nearby High-End Fitness Club
6 Blocks from Moscone Center

As a chain of modern boutique apartment hotels in Iran, Melal Hotel Group have been offering a warm welcome to guests from all over the world. According to the famous travel guide Lonely Planet excellent hospitality and services during the recent years have made it "undoubtedly the best accommodation in Tehran".

Melal Hotel Group

Designer: Salman Yaftabadi
Client: Melal Hotel Group
Location: Iran
Photographer: Salman Yaftabadi

Jamm
Apartment Hotel
هتل آپارتمان جم
Melal
Apartment Hotel
هتل آپارتمان ملل
Abtin
Apartment Hotel
هتل آپارتمان آبتین

MELAL
Hotel Group

Aasa
Welcome
MELAL
Hotel Group
Welcome
Useful information

MELAL
Hotel Group
Jamm Apartment Hotel
INVOICE

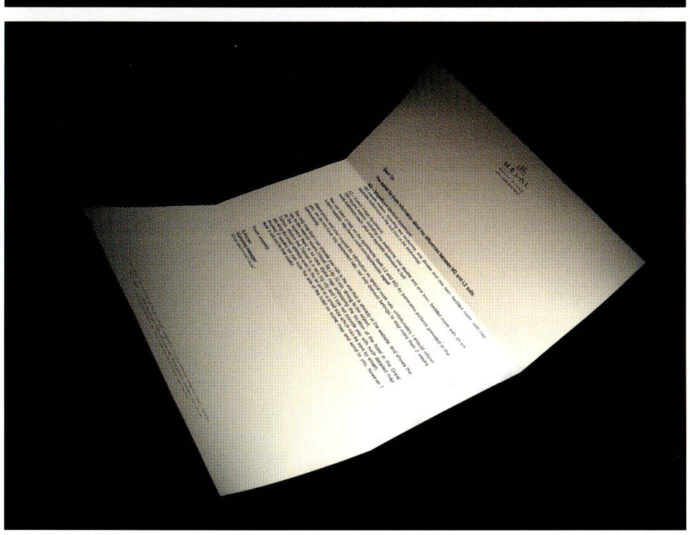

MELAL
Hotel Group
Body Shampoo
Shampoo
Soap

MELAL
Hotel Group
Body Lotion
www.melal.com
MELAL
Hotel Group
Body Shampoo
www.melal.com
MELAL
Hotel Group
Shampoo
www.melal.com

MELAL

I have had the privilege to create the entire visual image for the fabulous and classic Hotel Yöpuu and Restaurant Pöllöwaari. I began the project by designing the logo which symbolizes a tree, a word embedded in the name of the hotel. Over the years not only have I taken all the photographs, done all the visual and webpage design but I have also been in charge of compiling the restaurant's background music. I have to say, it has been quite an experience working with one of my dearest customers. My most recent creative project for them was designing the interior for one of the hotel rooms with my great friend and a promising furniture designer Antti Tuomi.

Hotel Yöpuu and Restaurant Pöllöwaari

Designer: Tero Ahonen

HOTELLI YÖPUU
RAVINTOLA PÖLLÖWAARI

Boutique Hotel
Yöpuu
RAVINTOLA PÖLLÖWAARI
PUH / TEL +358 (0)14 333 900
MYYNTIPALVELU@HOTELLIYOPUU.FI
WWW.HOTELLIYOPUU.FI
HOTELLI YÖPUU
RAVINTOLA PÖLLÖWAARI
YLIOPISTONKATU 23
40100 JYVÄSKYLÄ
FINLAND

Internacional Design Hotel is a small luxury and design hotel located in the centre of Lisbon that stands for a new hotel concept, providing a personal stay for each customer within four existing scenarios from the four corners of the world: Urban feeling, Tribal setting, Zen feeling and Pop atmosphere.

Suggestive photography, catch phrases and statements took inspiration from Lewis Carroll's "Alice in Wonderland", Andy Warhol's quotes, everyday expressions and proverbs.

Promotional brochure designed for Intenacional Design Hotel. In an A5 format this brochure combines high quality images with minimum information and stimulating statments having in mind the hotel's feeling and character.

Internacional Design Hotel

Design Agency: thisislove studio
Designer: Joana Areal and Inês Veiga
Client: Internacional Design Hotel

warm up!
zen
experience-
308 - 312

the world
fascinates me

0.
recepção //
reception

4.
408 - 412

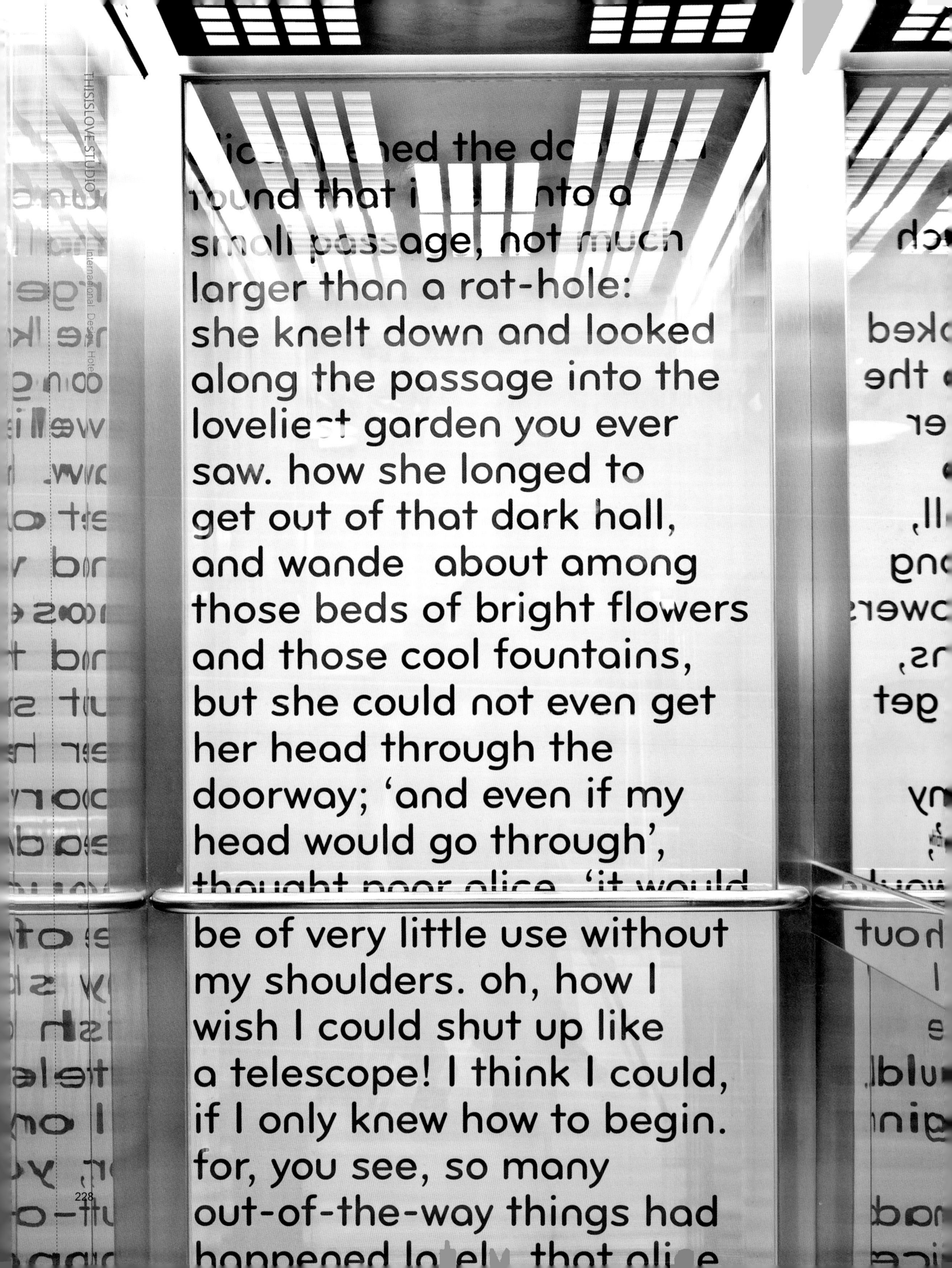
small passage, not much
larger than a rat-hole:
she knelt down and looked
along the passage into the
loveliest garden you ever
saw. how she longed to
get out of that dark hall,
and wande about among
those beds of bright flowers
and those cool fountains,
but she could not even get
her head through the
doorway; 'and even if my
head would go through',
be of very little use without
my shoulders. oh, how I
wish I could shut up like
a telescope! I think I could,
if I only knew how to begin.
for, you see, so many
out-of-the-way things had

inter-
nacional
design hotel
inter-
nacional
design hotel

inter-
nacional
design hotel

heaven
room

inter-
nacional
design hotel
Member of
slh.com
the world
fascinates me

The Sultan is a brand-new boutique hotel located at 101 Jalan Sultan, Singapore. Consisting of ten lovingly rebuilt conservation shop houses, The Sultan is the shiniest new gem in Kampong Glam.

The Sultan

Design Agency: Manic Design

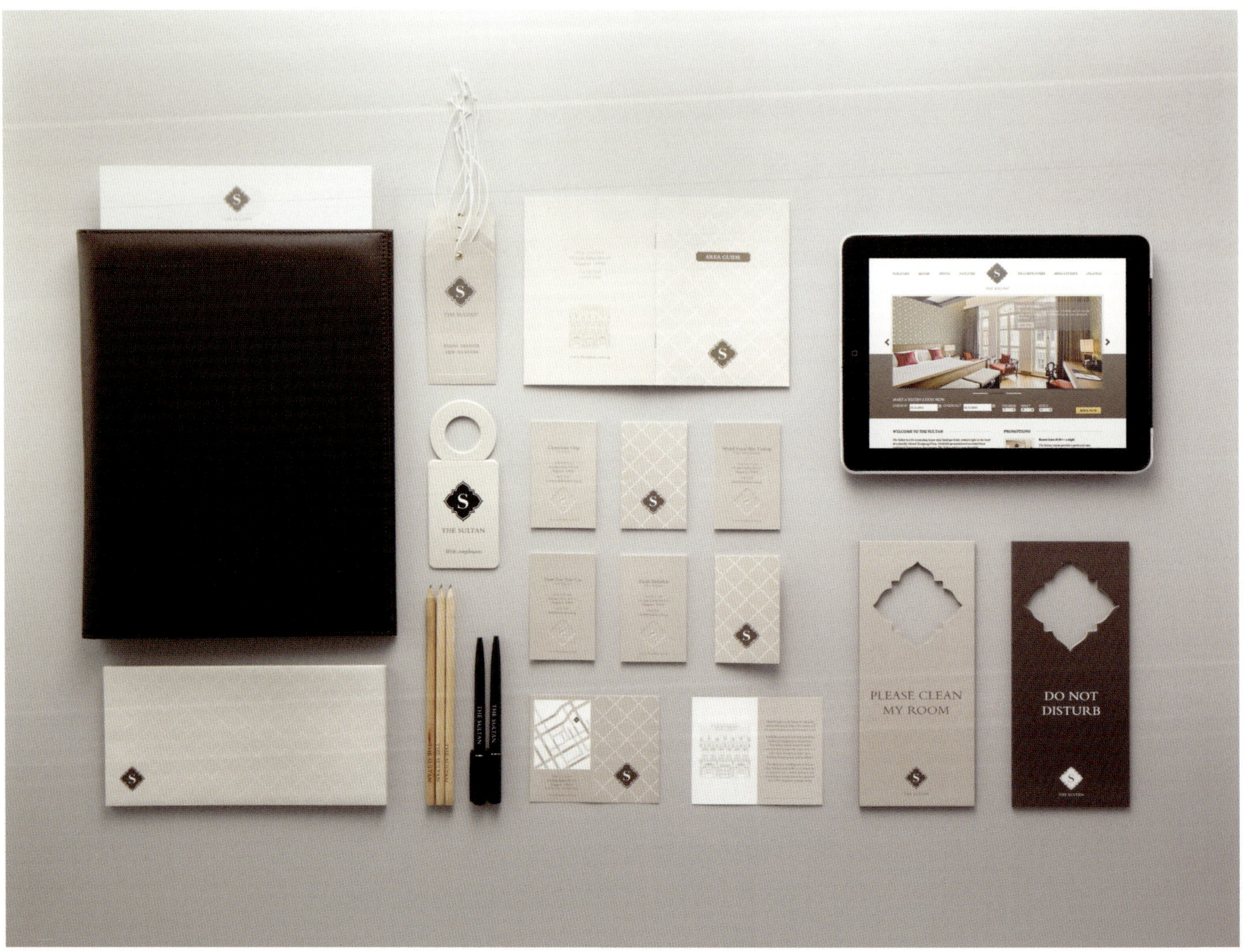

PLEASE CLEAN
MY ROOM
THE SULTAN
DO NOT
DISTURB
THE SULTAN

THE SULTAN
With compliments
Gant Tan Tian Cai
Zarah Abdullah
VICTORIA STREET
NORTH BRIDGE ROAD
BEACH ROAD
NICOLL HIGHWAY

THE SULTAN
S
THE SULTAN
THE SULTAN
THE SULTAN

TASTING SINGAPORE

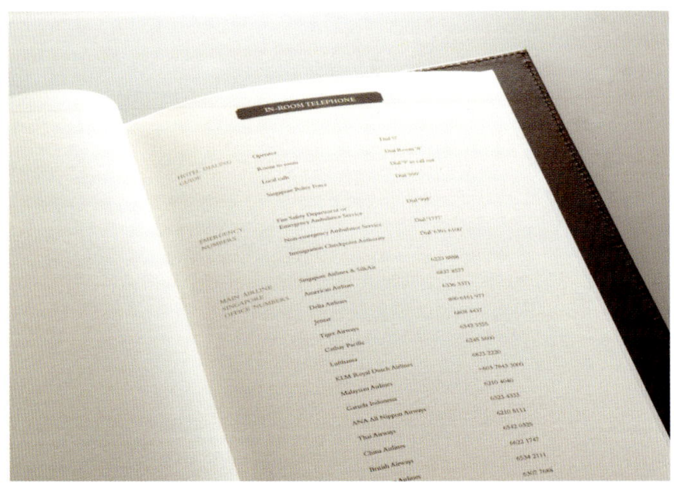
IN-ROOM TELEPHONE

SINGAPOREANS IN A NUTSHELL
KAMPONG GLAM

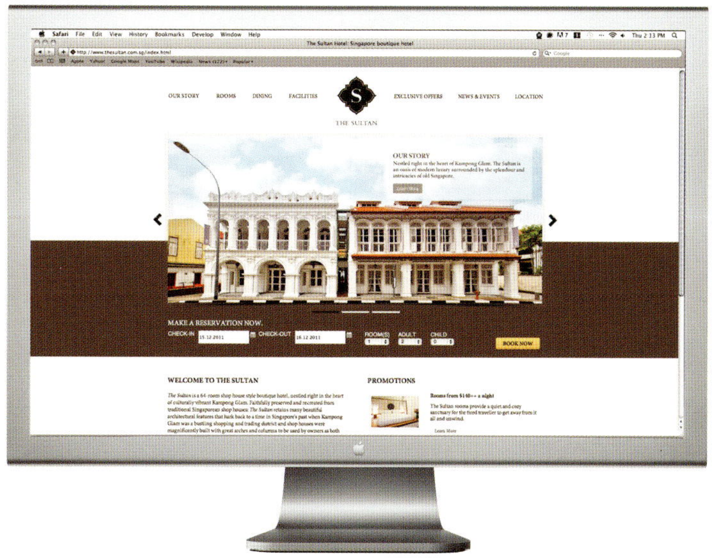
OUR STORY
ROOMS
DINING
FACILITIES
EXCLUSIVE OFFERS
NEWS & EVENTS
LOCATION
THE SULTAN
MAKE A RESERVATION NOW.
BOOK NOW
WELCOME TO THE SULTAN
PROMOTIONS

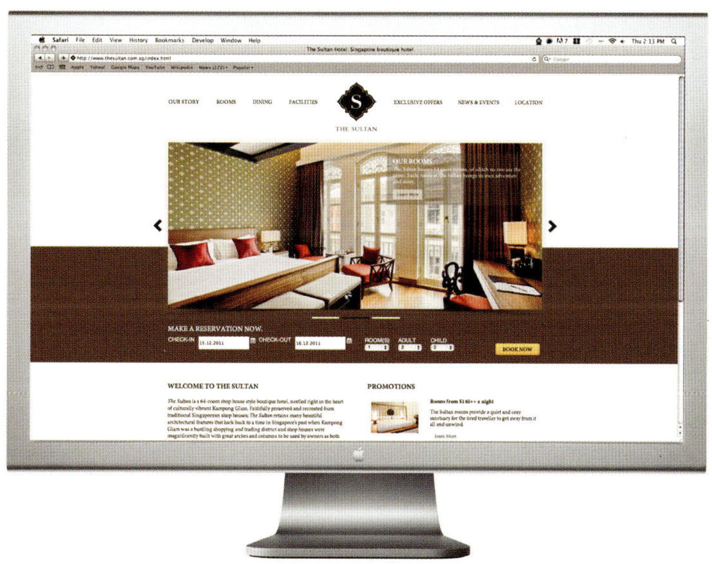
OUR STORY
ROOMS
DINING
FACILITIES
EXCLUSIVE OFFERS
NEWS & EVENTS
LOCATION
THE SULTAN
MAKE A RESERVATION NOW.
BOOK NOW
WELCOME TO THE SULTAN
PROMOTIONS

OUR STORY
ROOMS
DINING
FACILITIES
EXCLUSIVE OFFERS
NEWS & EVENTS
LOCATION
THE SULTAN
LOCATION

Beijing Gupeng Graphic Design Inc. was design the identity for Kailey hotel.

KAILEY HOTEL
凯 丽 酒 店

Kailey Hotel

Design Agency: Beijing Gupeng Graphic Design Inc.
Designer: Gupeng, Shixin
Art Director: GuPeng
Client: Kailey Hotel

KAILEY HOTEL

KAILEY HOTEL
凯 丽 酒 店

KAILEY HOTEL
Reserved

KELLY HOTEL
凯 丽 酒 店

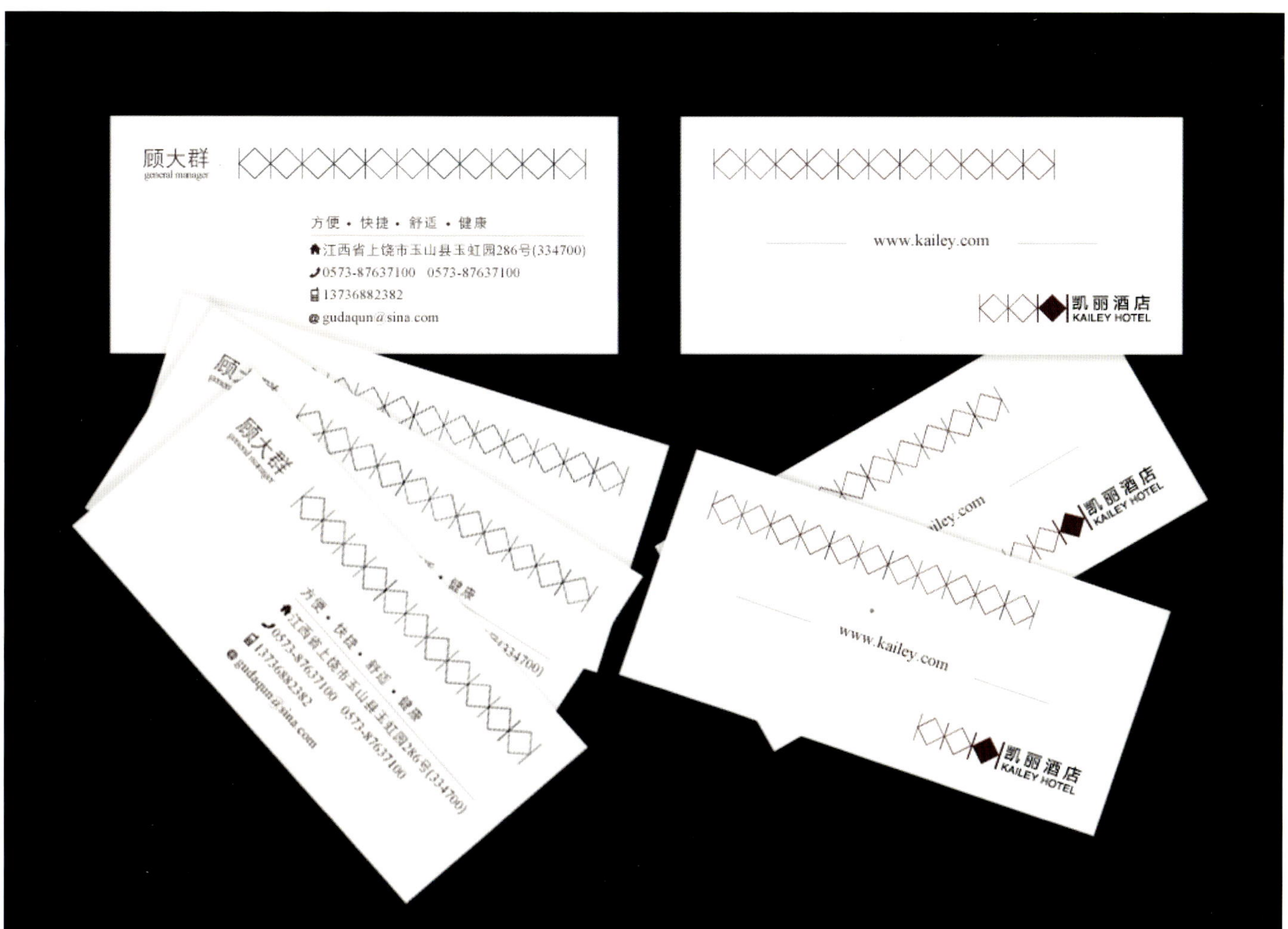
顾大群
general manager
方便 • 快捷 • 舒适 • 健康
江西省上饶市玉山县玉虹园286号(334700)
0573-87637100 0573-87637100
13736882382
gudaqun@sina.com
www.kailey.com
凯丽酒店
KAILEY HOTEL

On conditions that promote the hotel's quality to match with Radegast's spirit better, designer designed a series of package and promoted application. According to the scope and theme of application, designer achieved 'big effect' with 'small design', with different materials and expression way.

Radegast Hotel

Design Agency: Gollop Roch Creative Design
Designer: Kong Rongtao

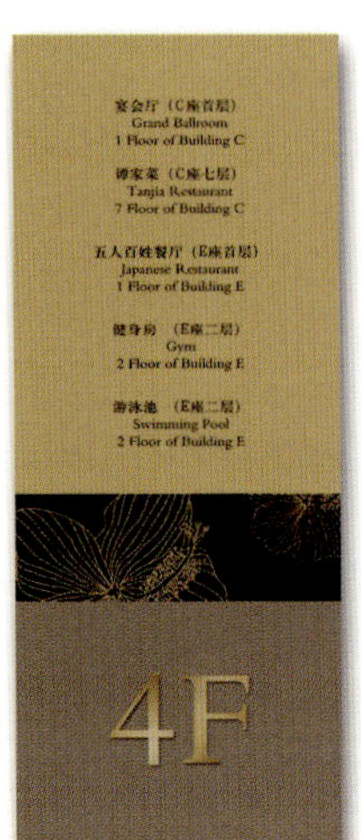

Yuan SPA
水疗中心

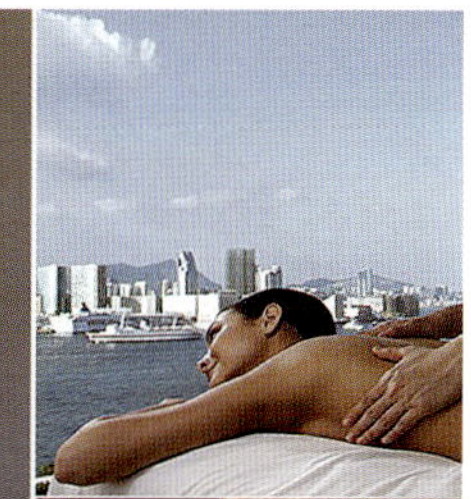

Radegast 瑞廷
欢迎卡
Welcome card

Radegast 瑞廷
欢迎卡
Welcome card

This corporate identity project was commissioned by the The Mirror Barcelona, a four star hotel and restaurant run by the two Michelin star winner, the iconic chef Paco Pérez.

The development consists of two parts; conceptualization and implementation. The essence of the project stems from the name establishment's "The Mirror", as that gives a concept and visual richness based on the duality, amplitude and proyection of the brand.

The brand work has tried to create graphic contexts that combine simplicity and sobriety, based on the mix of whites and silvers, complemented decisively by a sans serif typeface logo.

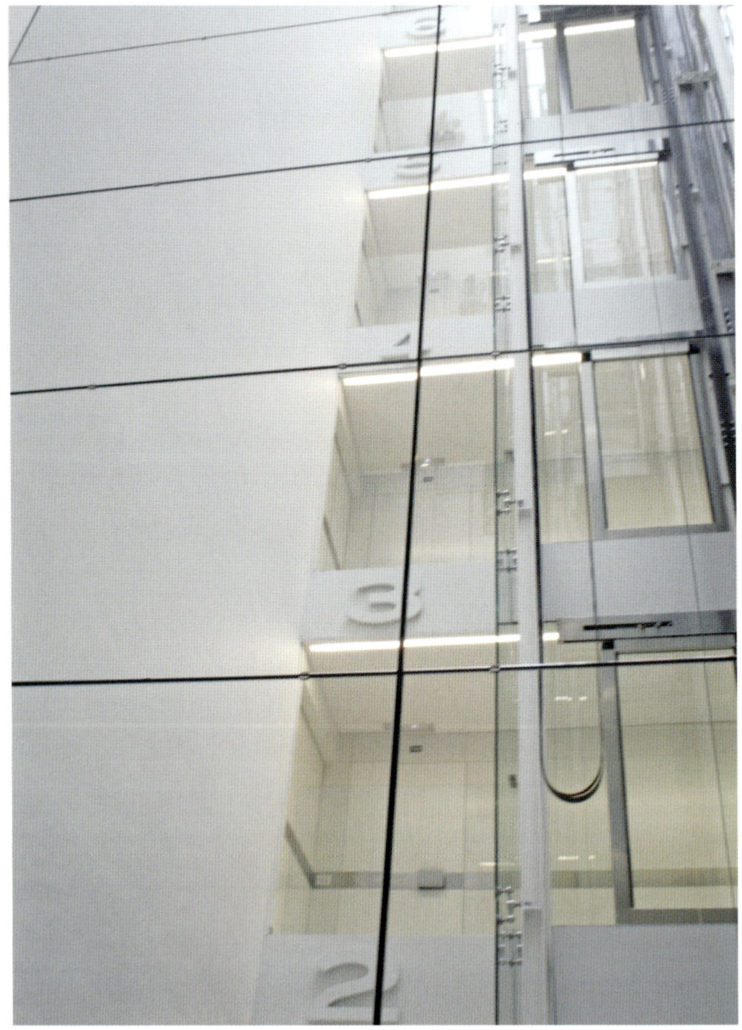

The Mirror Barcelona

Designer: Paqui Cuello, Lucía Herrador, Julia Laguarda
Architecture Agency: GCA Arquitectos Asociados
Client: Corporación Patrimonial Hotelera

EXIT

255

THE
MIRROR

THE
MIRROR
BARCELONA
Carrer Córcega, 255
08036 Barcelona
Tel.: +34 932 028 686
Fax: +34 932 028 684
info@themirrorbarcelona.com
www.themirrorbarcelona.com

THE
MIRROR
BARCELONA
RESTAURANT

RESTAURANT
MIRROR

THE
MIRROR
BARCELONA

THE
MIRROR
RESTAURANT

RESTAURANT
BARCELONA

VISUAL IMAGE DESIGN

CONTRIBUTOR

& SMITH

Based in East London & SMITH is a small design studio passionate about the craft and value of design. & SMITH work closely with their clients to achieve a full understanding of their business, ensuring that the work they produce engages and inspires their audience. Their work encompasses corporate identity, branding, print, web solutions, book design, signage and packaging.

& SMITH believe that being small and independent gives them the opportunity to provide each of their clients the hands-on attention to detail they deserve, and because there are no middlemen involved, their clients work directly with the designers from day one.

160over90

160over90 is a branding agency located in Philadelphia, Pennsylvania and Newport Beach, California. Part think tank, part design shop, 160over90 approaches every project with a unique perspective. 160over90's client list includes Nike, the Miami Dolphins, and Mercedes-Benz.

Accent Collective Inc.

Accent Collective is an independent creative firm based in Taipei, Taiwan. Driven by ideas and function, we explore possibilities looking to realize the full potential of brands. We find the distinctive accents of our clients and translate them into designed experiences.

Ada Rothenberg

Ada Rothenberg is an art director, designer and lecturer for communication design.

The studio specializes in branding, book and publication design. It focuses on cultural, educational and non-profit organizations.

The hotels featured here were renovated and reborn as concept-driven boutique hotels. Each of them delivers a unique experience.

The studio lives and works by its motto: Design for a Change.

Anais La Rocca

A New Yorker inside and out, Anais La Rocca graduated from The School of Visual Arts and now works in the city as an Art Director. She loves typography and has done a lot of travelling photographing and collecting type and design from around the world.

Amenábar & Yávar

Amenábar & Yávar is a design office based in Santiago de Chile. We work in the fields the of identity, exhibition, interiors, editorial design and strategic communication. Our commitment is to bring to our clients funtional results with a esthetically, always with a seal of excellence.

Bruketa&Žinić OM

Bruketa&Žinić OM consists of advertising agency Bruketa&Žinić OM Zagreb, Bruketa&Žinić OM Baku, brand consultants Brandoctor, digital agency Brlog and Brigada - design studio specialized in optimization of retail stores, product design and architecture.

Bruketa&Žinić OM Zagreb is one of the most award-winning advertising agencies in Southeastern Europe, with over 300 international awards, such as Art Directors Club New York, Epica, London International Awards, New York Festivals, Cresta, Clio, Effie, etc.

Bruketa&Žinić OM Baku is an Azerbaijani agency which officially opened its doors in early 2011, offering the complete range of services of the other Bruketa&Žinić OM agencies. It was co-founded by Bruketa&Žinić OM Zagreb and Moe Minkara.

Brandoctor is the first Croatian branding agency. It was founded by Davor Bruketa, Nikola Žinić, Anja Bauer Minkara and Moe Minkara in 2004, as a response to a growing need for branding in Croatia. The agency consists of top brand consultants, naming consultants, designers, market analysts and brand implementers. Brandoctors are experts educated in Croatia and abroad, experienced in building and designing foreign, as well as Croatian brands.

Brlog is a digital creative agency founded in 2009, which deals with the creation of digital services related to the interaction between a brand and a consumer (digital brand promotion).

Brigada is a studio specialized in the design and optimization of retail stores, product design and architecture. It was founded in 2010 by Bruketa&Žinić OM and Damjan Geber, B.Arch.

Beijing Gupeng Graphic Design Inc.

Beijing Gupeng Graphic Design Inc. is focusing on research and development in new brand image field, while dedicating in diverse performance and construction of the brand image. Based on the idea of tailor-made, the company is aiming at creating a unique brand visual execution. Design fields include: brand image design, brand promotion design, brand terminal environment design, experiments on new visual exploration, etc. Works have been awarded by national and international industry and published in various professional brochures and yearbooks. They have been widely recognized by the market. Through close professional cooperation and information exchange with different places in Asia, brand new ideas and prolific resources are provided in company's brand design services.

Carol Rivello

Carol Rivello is a graphic designer who loves to work with web design, art direction and illustration. Now she lives in Florianópolis, a pretty island located in the south of Brazil, and works as a freelancer. She love pigs, and has more than 300 of them. Carol also loves: Internet, Music, Traveling, Movies, TV Shows, Illustration, Sketch Books, Motion Design, Home Decor, T-shirts, Pigs, Chocolate, Ice cream , Birds, Clouds, Sun, Sea and almost everything from the 80's.

Carrie Anne Seaver

Carrie Anne Seaver is the owner and Creative Director of Anemone Design, an award-winning boutique studio in Washington, DC. She is passionate about creating visual identities in print and online that are as intelligent as they are attractive. Her clients range from restaurants, hotels and chefs to publishers, fashion designers and nightclubs. And as the wife of a chef, she has a unique insight into the restaurant industry.

Cesar Corpus

With a solid 4 years of experience, Cesar Corpus is a graphic design freelancer specializing in print, identity, branding and web design.

Cesar Corpus has a distinctive approach to communication and design, as a result of working at studios such as Boccalatte and experience in the music industry (including servicing clients such as Fuzzy and Jam).

Cesar's qualifications include a Bachelor of Design degree with the University of New South Wales (COFA) and the Bauhaus University Weimar, Germany and has undergone AWARD school.

"Having a background that is conceptually driven and multi-disciplined, I'm a strong believer in producing fresh work that conveys a message with a purpose. My creativity is influenced by lifestyle and life experiences".

Charlotte Warren

I am Charlotte Warren, a Graphic Design student very soon to finish my BA degree at The Leeds College Of Art. I have always been passionate about design with my main interests including typography, layout, brand identity and packaging design. As well as design, I have a passion for food. This often tends to be a focus within my work, mainly in the areas of packaging and branding. I like to see myself as creative, committed and most of all, a perfectionist. I'm always focused yet love to learn something new. I enjoy a challenge meaning I always try to push myself to make the most of things.

CODO Design

CODO Design is a two-man Indianapolis Branding & Design firm dedicated to improving the community. Cody Fague and Isaac Arthur graduated from Herron School of Art and Design in May, 2009 and founded this business on two deeply held beliefs:

1. We believe we can create better design by directly involving our clients in the creative process.

2. We believe we can improve the community through design.

We've spent the last two years developing our Hands-on Branding process, tailoring it to expertly tease out the knowledge and vision found within passionate, creative nonprofit folks and restaurateurs.

Cristina Jucan

A Romanian national who has degrees in both arts and languages, Cristina Jucan is a graphic designer and jewelry designer now based in Memphis, TN (US). Her passion for design comes from her innate curiosity and desire to communicate ideas by any medium necessary. She believes each project must begin with lots of research, to develop a better understanding of the client's needs and background, while suspending all preconceptions to allow the project to speak with its own voice and create deeper meaning within itself. This search, she feels, leads to more rewarding, authentic designs and a greater relationship between her, the client, and the project.

Danielle Dunn Creative Agency

Nick is a highly motivated and passionate individual with over seven years experience in the creative industry. An established, experienced designer and ambitious entrepreneur with a broad design/marketing background across brand, print, advertising, web and multimedia. He has had the pleasure of working with a wide range of top regional and national businesses as well as international brands including Max Factor, Olay, Pantene, Hugo Boss, H&S, Mazda and Ministry of Sound to name but a few.

Now MD of Studio Precept and Creative Director at DDCA, Nick manages the studio at Social HQ providing all creative and strategic direction to the team. When he's not scribbling or at his mac, you'll find him swooning with clients and suppliers or calmly tending to the general running of the business. Popular with all of his clients, Nick is personable, knowledgeable and renowned for his conceptual thinking, attention to detail and his ability to get the balance right between form and function.

Deuce Design

Founded in 2000 by Sophie Tatlow and Bruce Slorach, the studio is committed to creative and unique design outcomes. We are dedicated and passionate individuals who seek to provide successful and creative communication solutions for our clients. Working across various sectors and disciplines, we frequently collaborate with other consultants, architects, artists and creatives. Our projects range from the small boutique brand projects for colleagues to extensive environmental branding, communications strategies and interpretive and wayfinding solutions for public domain.

The studio prides itself on its energetic and creative team and its ability to being able to work across all project types and sizes.

Elever

Elever is a 360° design studio based in Milan, founded in 2001.

Specialized in corporate identity, digital design and mobile applications, Elever mixes creative passion with technology and works closely with the clients to give them the best solutions to communicate.

Ennis Perry Creative

Ennis Perry Creative is a branding and communication agency based in Melbourne, Australia. We create unique brands through genuine innovation & creativity.

Our relationship with branding and communication started more than 15 years ago, ever since we have been creating value and building demand for our clients through unique & tailored creativity.

We help our clients navigate markets & opportunities, we direct all creativity and ideas through workshops & strategic planning, our process starts with a focus on strategy, resulting in solutions that are considered, intelligent and engaging.

Our commitment to what we promise is evident in the defining areas of our business - strategic and creative process, investment in our clients' brands, and living and participating in the markets on which we focus.

Enrique Gonzalo

Enrique Gonzalo is a Graphic Designer and Art Director located in Bilbao, Spain. After finishing studies in Law-Economics at Deusto University in Bilbao, Enrique followed his passion for art and visual communication by deciding to start a career based in creativity.

In order to achieve that, he moved to New York City where he graduated with honours at the prestigious Pratt Institute School of Design.

While living in New York, he worked in several studios gaining experience that led him to a full time position as an Art Director at Ogilvy and Mather NY, where he completed five years of online and offline campaigns for clients such as IBM, SAP, Siebel, Perrier, Motorola and Cisco, among others.

In 2008, after ten years in New York, he decided to establish himself in Spain, and work as a freelancer Designer.

Elissa Shapiro

Elissa Shapiro Design is based in New York City. Elissa is a graduate of Pennsylvania State University and Parsons The New School for Design. She has degrees in both Marketing and Graphic Design. Prior to her career in graphic design, she worked for several years in the music industry as band management (Bon Jovi) and in concert promotion (AEG Live). She has worked on a variety of projects including museum exhibitions, identities, publications, and web design. Some of her work includes The New York Public Library, The Children's Museum of Manhattan and Tribeca Film Festival.

Erika Magallon

Erika Magallon is a graphic designer who has a love for nature, a passion for creativity, and a joy for creating brands and experimenting with all types of packaging. As a hobby, she also likes to learn and explore new heights.

Erika Magallon graduated from the BFA Graphic Design Program at California Sate University of Long Beach in 2011 and lives in Los Angeles, California.

Filip Kokoszynski

Filip Kokoszynski, a Polish designer and web developer with 7 years of work experience is responsible for the branding and the website project. Filip began his career at the age of 18, since then he mainly concentrated on: brand identity, from separate logos to creating the overall corporate identity, as well as on website design. He also cooperated with the largest Polish radio station - RMF FM and with the biggest Polish press newspaper - Gazeta Wyborcza (Agora S.A.). In 2010 Filip opened his own creative agency IDEA07, of which he is the art director, dealing mainly with naming, branding and website design.

The characteristic features of his style are minimalism, playing with typography and excellent colour selection for each of his projects. As for websites design, Filip tends to maintain simplicity, from the user's perspective, while keeping all communication functions of the given project. He also enjoys designing BTL advertisements, in which he likes to use unconventional forms of communication.

Foreign Policy Design Group

Foreign Policy Design Group is a team of idea makers & story tellers who help clients and brands realize and evolve their brands with creative and strategic deployment of traditional terrestrial channel & digital media channels. Helmed by Creative Directors Yah-Leng Yu and Arthur Chin, the group works on a good smorgasbord of projects ranging from creative/art direction and design, branding, brand strategy, digital strategy, strategic research and marketing campaign services for luxury fashion and lifestyle brands, fast-moving consumer goods brands, arts and cultural institution as well as think tank consultancies.

Graphasel Design Studio

Our team was established in 2003 at the Hungarian University of Fine Arts. The mission is to provide our clients with visual concepts conceived with the highest artistic quality.

We always want to create more than mere design, and strive to find the best possible means of implementation.

Our goal is to build well-functioning visual communications projects that have as much creative appeal as purpose. We are open to new challenges that require unique graphic design solutions on online and offline platforms alike.

Gollop Roch Creative Design

Founded in 2010, Gollop Roch Creative Design can provide identity design for hotel, logo design, VI design, pictorial design, package design, business exhibition, website design and other design services.

Lea Zupančič

My name is Lea Zupančič and I came from Ljubljana (Slovenia). I am studying Graphic and Interactive Communication - master program in Ljubljana. In my spare time i am working as a graphic designer. If there is some extra spare time i create something for myself or my friends. From all I love illustration the most.

Design of a brand 18sedem3 was made in association with Memoinstitut - agency for creative research (http://www.memo.si/) who developed the brand.

Indelible Design

Indelible Design is a Vancouver based graphic design studio that makes marks in branding, print, environmental design, and web solutions. Indelible focuses on communicative design with attention to process, message, production, format, type & layout.

We are committed to fostering engaging client-designer relationships by listening and delivering visual creativity to the highest possible quality. We believe clean & simple solutions are usually the best.

Jay Fletcher

For the past decade Jay Fletcher has been working in Charleston as a graphic designer, illustrator, and art director. In 2004, as a means of burning off unused creativity, a budding freelance career took root as a late-night side gig. Kegs of coffee were brewed, momentum built, and now J Fletcher Design has a stable of transformed clients and shelves of recognition from some of the design world's most prominent voices.

Javas Lehn

Javas Lehn is a Design Director currently living and working in NYC. He works in the broadest range of media, including: identity, interactive, interior, photography and film. Through both design and art direction, he strives to create innovative and conceptually new work that emotionally resonates with the audience.

Javas has collaborated with artists, fashion designers, photographers and product designers, drawing inspiration from a broad range of interests that span mid-century modern furniture, skateboard and snowboard culture, fashion and a deep appreciation for architecture.

His artistic interests shape his personal as well as his professional life. Javas spends his free time capturing moments through portraiture with his Leica, creating short films, and drawing creative inspiration from his travels around the world.

Jennifer Cordova

Jennifer Cordova is an Art Director and Graphic designer in New York City. She specializes in branding and identity for fashion and beauty.

Karenina "Nina" Simmons

Everyone has a place, a goal or destiny and Nina's desire is to combine words and images together to create designs that speak to whoever sees them. She is a firm believer that Passion Equals Success. If one desires something nothing should stop them from acquiring it. Nina seeks out new and innovative technology, possess the ability to grasp concepts quickly and gather facts and materials effectively and efficiently. While sometimes reserved, She can be aggressive and competitive when goals require, and always decisive. Nina has learned the value of marketing strategy, artistic innovation, effective management, print and electronic continuity, professional acumen and team building.

Since 2005, Karenina "Nina" Simmons has been a freelance graphic designer. Her clientele includes a diverse array of businesses and organizations, both large and small. She currently works for a design and marketing firm, where she has designed, produced and managed projects; including logos, catalogs, posters, and websites. She hopes to go into business for herself. She enjoys the creative challenge, working directly with her clients, and pushing herself to produce the best work possible.

Knoed Creative

Knoed is the creative studio of Kim Knoll and Kyle Eertmoed. Located in Chicago, they provide creative strategy, design and development to entrepreneurs, small businesses and organizations of all shapes and sizes. Whether it's a mom and pop shop, a highly acclaimed agency or a Fortune 100 company, they deliver the same integrity, passion and dedication to a great concept and smart design. Their work has been recognized in publications such as Communication Arts, Print Magazine and HOW Magazine and has been published in books by Rockport Publishers, Princeton Architectural Press and Dopress Books.

Line Arlander

Line Arlander was educated from Denmark Design School in 2005 and the Graphic Arts Institute in 2008, with a bachelor in graphic design, and be employed at Scandinavian Design Lab since 2008.

Scandinavian Design Lab is an independent design agency based in Copenhagen, Denmark with representation in Shanghai, China, working with a focus on creative and strong solutions for packaging clients, fashion agencies and corporate identities for large companies in both Denmark and China.

Line Arlander's personal focus has always been within packaging design (mainly foodstuff) and development of corporate identities. It's always interesting and exciting to work on the 2D visual expression for a new client on-screen, but the point of truth, and where the real satisfaction for me as a designer emerges, is when the final design is brought to life; when the senses are evoked, by choosing the right materials and printing techniques and the implementation of a new identity is exactly how you imagined. This is where design really matters and makes a difference for the client.

LoSiento

After starting his career in Industrial Design at Escola de Disseny Elisava (Barcelona), Borja Martínez moved to London in 1999 to study Graphic Design at the London College of Printing (today, London College of Communication).

He returns to Barcelona and, in 2005, founds LoSiento, where he starts developing different Graphic Design and art direction projects. Nowadays, LoSiento gathers a team of 5 professionals and continues to work in design projects from the fields of corporative, packaging, editorial and carrying out personal projects as well.

The studio is especially interested in taking over identity projects as a whole. Its main feature of LoSiento's work is a physical approach to the graphic solutions, resulting in a field where graphic and industrial designs go hand by hand, always searching for alliances with the artisans' process.

Matilda Svensson

Matilda Svensson is a graphic designer from Stockholm in Sweden. During the days she works as an art director of a magazine, during nights and weekends she takes photos and freelance. She loves typography, beautiful photos and groundbreaking use of different styles mixed together into something new. With a background in print and typography, a bachelor from the School of Arts and Communication in Malm , several summers spent at design agencies in Paris, and almost two years at magazine publisher in Stockholm she has a broad knowledge from a variety of fields within graphic design.

Manic Design

We are an award-winning creative agency with a portfolio of work that ranges from websites and online campaigns to advertising and branding.

The studio was founded in 1999 with the belief that good design always includes both creativity and communication. A piece of work that looks great but fails to speak to its audience is not good design. We have embraced this and cemented it into our culture and our work.

Mateusz Piekarski

Mateusz Piekarski is a Polish graphic designer, living in London, working at popcorn and co-founder of Odnowa.

Meter Industries

Meter Industries, started by award winning creative director Marty Weiss, has specialized in brand make-over and brand launches for many of our clients, including A/X Armani Exchange, Grand Central Terminal, Waterworks and Sobieski Vodka to name a few. Our aim is to create unique visual, verbal and behavioral language that is both visceral and powerful to anyone exposed to a brand - from employees to shareholders; to the trade and consumers. Key capabilities include strategic and creative consultation, logo and brand identity, advertising, digital and web design, packaging, point of sale, collateral, etc.

Medina & Grisolía

Medina & Grisolía was born in 2004 in the city of Mérida, Venezuela, as a professional collaboration between Graphics Designers Carmen Grisolía and Jhonatan Medina. We are an independent creative studio with global vison. We specialize in creating powerful, meaningful and professional communication designs in areas such as brand identity and development, art direction, packaging, printed matter, art projects, exhibitions, illustration and fashion.

M&G works with national and international clients and projects covering a wide variety of visual Communications problems. We believe in simplicity. We believe in collaboration. We believe in originality. We believe in design.

Michelle Gadeken

Michelle Gadeken is a graphic designer born and raised in the Pacific Northwest. Throughout her creative life she has developed a fascination for the thin and dynamic line between art and design. She has enjoyed the many rich and fortunate opportunities she has had, to explore and learn in a vast array of creative mediums. In 2011 she earned her BA in design from Western Washington University, located in Bellingham, Washington. She looks forward to a long and active life in the creative field.

Nicholas Aufiero

Nicholas is a Phoenix-based designer, runner and chef. He grew up in Springfield, Virginia and graduated from the Savannah College of Art and Design (SCAD), with a Bachelor of Fine Arts degree in Graphic Design.

Nicole Fischer

Nicole Fischer is a graphic designer/art director currently working in Portland, Oregon as a freelancer. She's worked on a variety of projects in her 10-plus year career, from identity and print design to web and interactive. Nicole's favorite part of design is solving her clients' problems in a visually compelling way.

Nicole started Seedling Design a year and a half ago and has loved running her own studio. Her array of clients ranges from Fortune 100 companies to local photography studios--a variety that allows for compelling creative exploration to come up with the right business solutions.

Nicole's work is influenced by the city in which she lives, and she pulls daily inspiration from the nature of the Pacific Northwest.

NOISE 13

Founded in Jan. of 2000, Noise 13 has been a source for lifestyle branding and design both locally in San Francisco and nationally. We have clients in the Bay Area, Hawaii, Seattle, San Diego, New York, Luxemburg and Sweden. To better serve our East Coast clients we have partnered with a project management team in New York for day-to-day collaboration.

Noise 13's current expertise lies in full scale branding projects for lifestyle businesses. We love the business to consumer connection and aim to strengthen our client's brands and well and keep their existing customers happy. In any lifestyle industry, existing happy and loyal customers are the best marketing. Our capabilities span from brand strategy, identify design, print design, marketing design, website design & development, email marketing, interface & UI design, as well as packaging, and environment design to complete the brand experience. We partner with writers, social media & SEO companies, photographers, and illustrators to enhance a brand's overall message and visibility. In many cases we are more like partners with our clients and grow with them and their brand.

The Noise 13 team, either while at Noise or in previous positions, has expertise working with hospitality, food & beverage, non-profit, pets, beauty & health, fashion and music, among others. From re-branding Personality Hotels corporate and their individual hotels, to branding and designing for new Pets Co. stores and their in-house merchandise, to winery brands and restaurants, the Noise 13 team is the strategy, design, and usually the customer. We do not work with brands we do not believe in or would not recommend to friends.

North55

North55 is an independent, multi-discipline creative agency established in 2001 to offer international standards of branding and design to clients in the UAE and the wider Middle East region. Our clients include Emirates Airline, One & Only Resorts, Masdar, the European Tour and the Jumeirah Group.

Paqui Cuello

My name is Paqui Cuello, born and grown in Santa Coloma (Barcelona, Spain). I studied graphic design to make a Brand Identity Master in Elisava School in Barcelona afterwards. My professional career was developed though my stay in three design agencies in the Catalonian city to dedicate to freelance projects for Spain and Chile afterward.

Design is part of my life. I love the challenges which offer the opportunity of growing and enriching my knowledge and professional experience.

Paperview Design

Paperview is a design studio and concept lab specialising in print media.

From our offices in Beirut, we have collaborated with a roster of international and regional clients.

Our services include: Corporate branding, Identity creation and development, and multimedia design. Paperview also has a highly successful track record in the restaurant sector, where its experience has translated into some of the most well known restaurants, lounges and clubs in the region's nightlife.

Our clients run on a broad spectrum from architects, interior designers, jewellery designers, restaurants, bars, nightclubs, hotels, universities, Beauty lounges, delivery concepts, to IT companies, NGO's and pharmaceuticals.

Rosalind Roongseang

My name is Rosalind Roongseang, and I'm a designer living and working in New York. Outside of my full time job, I enjoy freelancing and working on a variety of work from website design to restaurant branding. I specialize in integrated branding systems and experiences, and believe that a strong branding is at core of a successful business. I've been a designer for 5 years and am looking forward to many more.

Rubber Design

Rubber Design is a small, award-winning, multi-disciplinary design studio located in San Francisco, California. Principals Jacquie Van Keuren and Will Yarbrough founded the firm in 2001 with a mission of creating an environment that fosters the same high caliber of work for clients large or small. Whether working with a local startup opening a single location or an established global bank, they offer the same focused attention to a brand.

With an emphasis on branding, they can just as easily take a business from the ground up or steward an existing brand through its next phase. The team at Rubber Design prides themselves on offering flexible solutions that carry clients through years of growth and that effectively communicates across all media.

Rui Dias

Rui Dias doesn't believe in perfection. He is always looking for problems in things, taking pre-established notions apart and thinking of how to make everything better. He is a young self-taught designer from Portugal with a lot of energy and many graphic design, art direction and photography projects under his belt. He approaches every new challenge with respect and never fails to deliver beautiful solutions and functional results.

Runar Lillegård

Stilk is the portfolio of Runar Lillegård, Art Director and Designer. Lives and works in Stavanger, Norway. Specialized in brand identities, design for print, packaging and interactive Medias.

He is currently working as a graphic designer at Ghost Design. The submitted work is done while working at procontra advertising agency in Stavanger, Norway.

Salman Yaftabadi

Salman Yaftabadi is an Iranian designer and design director, working as graphic designer since 2000. He is the Member of Iranian Graphic Designer's Society (IGDS), Specialized in brand identity design has advised many of the Iranian's leading enterprises on identity, branding, communication and related matters. His works has been published in numerous international magazines and books.

Sérgio Alves

An emerging young designer based in the city of Porto, northern Portugal. Sergio's designs are not limited to a specific school or idea, but rather often based on art & craft or use of organic materials within the design process. Each project may differ greatly from the next as he experiments with new mediums and allows each project to dictate the best way to communicate.

Sergio's inspirations can be found in other national and international designers, as well as in typical national visual stimuli such as craft, gastronomy, national culture and playful use of typography.

His main focuses have been on creating posters for cultural events, which allow for greater experimentation and creativity. He also has some projects with editorial design and corporate identity.

Susannah Briggs

Susannah Briggs is a graphic designer living and working in Philadelphia. Good graphic design makes her weak in the knees, so it's only right that she's mostly found huddled over her monitor, obsessing over every last detail of a project.

She loves anything handmade, and her work mostly focuses on publishing and packaging. On the off chance that she's not glued to her computer, she can be found reading everything in sight, throwing board game parties for her friends and trying new restaurants in Philadelphia.

Tero Ahonen

Tero Ahonen is a graphic designer, photographer and a creative designer living in Jyväskylä, Finland. Tero is known for his work with various Finnish musicians and bands such as Husky Rescue and the cult classic 22-Pistepirkko. His promo photography has been used in magazines all over the world. His wide range of references includes such prestigious institutions as Sibelius Academy and The Finnish Academy of Fine Arts. Tero's style is a mixture of strong ideas and stories which are communicated through striking and timeless design. Tero describes his working methods by saying: "In the beginning of each project I clear my mind and take it on as if it were my first".

thisislove studio

thisislove is a Lisbon based multidisciplinary design studio focused on communication design and experimental media projects.

This is Love works in collaboration with visual artists, architects, art curators, fashion designers, photographers, marketing strategists and many other individual talents.

thisislove is Joana Areal, Maria João Soromenho, Sofia Cardita, Inês Veiga and Nuno Sequeira.

Toormix

Toormix is a Barcelona-based design studio specialising in branding, art direction, creativity and graphic design, set up in 2000 by Ferran Mitjans and Oriol Armengou. Toormix is specialized in corporate identity, editorial, print, web and communication projects for a wide variety of clients, from small graphic pieces to global branding and communication projects.

In his career over 11 years of the studio they have worked with clients such as Desigual, Camper, MTV España, Spain USA Foundation, H10 Hotels, Spanish Ministry of Culture, Barcelona City Council, Pull & Bear and chef José Andrés among others.

Transplant

Transplant offers effective design solutions for public interior spaces from productive workspaces, to restaurants and hotels. The studio is dedicated to give each design a sense of meaning and personality. Integrating innovative materials into the processes, Transplant is aiming for sustainable design practice.

Birgitta Ralston and Alexandre Bau founded the studio in Paris in 2001. In 2007 Transplant's creative space opened on the shore of a Norwegian fjord.

UXUS

Founded in Amsterdam 2003 by George Gottl, Oliver Michell and Erika Gottl, UXUS is an international award wining design consultancy specializing in Retail, Architecture & Interiors, Hospitality, Brand Identity & Communication, and Strategic Concept Development.

At UXUS it all starts with collaboration, our name reflects that idea:

UXUS means "You Times Us".

UXUS creates "Brand Poetry": Artistic solutions for commercial needs. Our methodology fuses together Art and Design producing the perfect balance between emotional connection and commercial results. Design gives function, Art gives meaning, and Poetry expresses the essence.

"UXUS crafts brand experiences that people fall in love with."

UXUS has offices in Europe and the US with an international team of Designers, Project Managers and Strategists working together to create "Brand Poetry", a fusion of art and design to create new brand experiences.

Vingervlug

Vingervlug is a Hamburg-based design studio founded in 2011 with years of freelance experience. We evolve strong visual concepts that create excitement, we work in a multidisciplinary way and have a lot of fun. Vingervlug loves typographies.

Viviane Mosso

Viviane Mosso is an Italian graphic designer.

She has lived in France and works in Italy, United Kingdom and Czech Republic, places which influence her design approach. Her background is multidisciplinary and furthermore developed in academic graphic and communication studies.

Her works are based on creative concepts and usability, proposing an emotional and iconological impact.

With a predilection for patterns and typography, she covers projects of identity, branding, packaging and collateral design areas.

ARTPOWER

Acknowledgements

We would like to thank all the designers and companies who made a significant contribution to the compilation of this book. Without them, this project would not have been possible. We would also like to thank many other people whose names do not appear in the credits, but who provided valuable input and support for the project from the start to its completion.

Future Editions

If you would like to contribute to future Artpower publications, please email your details to: info@artpower.com.cn.